War Clouds on the Horn of Africa: A Crisis for Détente

Tom J. Farer

CARNEGIE ENDOWMENT FOR INTERNATIONAL PEACE
NEW YORK   WASHINGTON, D.C.

I.S.B.N. 0-87003-006-X

Library of Congress Catalog Card Number: 76-29872

Printed in the United States of America.

To my Mother who keeps a liberal's faith, to Mika who also felt on the Horn's sere plains a glorious freedom of the heart, and to my children, Dima and Paola, who by their way of being in the world, help me to sustain the fragile belief that it is worth struggling to shape the future.

Contents

Foreword   vi

Acknowledgement   ix

Introduction   1

Part One: Ethiopia and Eritrea

1. Ethiopia   5
   THE SETTING   5
   THE PRESENT AS HISTORY   8
   AFTER THE FALL OF THE LION   11

2. Eritrea   20
   THE MAKING OF A STATE   20
   THE SHORT, UNHAPPY LIFE OF FEDERATION   26
   TOWARD NATIONAL LIBERATION   29

3. After the Revolution: National Socialism   37
   NATIONALISM: CONCILIATION CONFOUNDED   37
   AUTHORITARIAN SOCIALISM: REFORM BY BAYONET   42

Part Two: Ethiopia and the Somalis

4. The Roots of Conflict   49
   THE LAND AND PEOPLE   49
   THE COLONIAL PARTITIONS   53

5. Independence: A Partial Victory   73
   FREEDOM AND ITS DISCONTENTS   73
   MUTILATION OF THE PAN-SOMALI DREAM   77
   DEMOCRACY'S END   89

6. Somalia Under the Junta   93
   NATIONAL SOCIALISM   93
   DEFENSE AND FOREIGN POLICY   97

Part Three: A Policy Perspective

7. The Geopolitical Context: The Indian Ocean   105
   SOVIET INTERESTS   105

CONTENTS

SOVIET STRATEGIC SUPERIORITY? 110
A SOVIET BLOCKADE? 114
A PLAUSIBLE THREAT TO WESTERN INTERESTS? 116
POLICY IMPLICATIONS 118

8. The Geopolitical Context: Eritrea, Israel and the Red Sea 125
THE DUAL THREATS 125
THE OPTIONS IN ERITREA 130

9. Peaceful Settlement on the Horn: The Margin of Policy 136
ERITREA 136
SOMALIA 139

Epilogue: The Phenomenology of Crisis 152

Bibliography 154

List of Maps

The Horn of Africa:
International Boundaries xii

The Horn of Africa:
Provincial Boundaries Facing page 5

The Horn of Africa:
International Boundaries 1888-1960 Facing page 49

The Red Sea and the Persian Gulf Facing page 105

Foreword

By the summer of 1976 two developments had called world attention to the unfolding political and human crisis on the Horn of Africa. In January, 1976, the Ethiopian government distributed to African chiefs of state then meeting in Addis Ababa a thirty-nine-page memorandum entitled "War Clouds in the Horn of Africa." The document's purpose was to alert African governments to the growing tension between Ethiopia and Somalia. The memorandum documented a growing number of border incidents between the two countries and concluded that Somalia "has made a decision to go to war against Ethiopia immediately."

A few months later, the government in Addis Ababa stunned the world by taking the initial steps to organize a peasant invasion of the rebellious province of Eritrea. The success of the Moroccan government in annexing part of the Spanish Sahara by sending hundreds of thousands of ordinary Moroccans spilling into the adjacent colony may well have emboldened the Ethiopian authorities to strike with similar recklessness. In any event, in late spring, 1976, the Ethiopian government armed thousands of simple peasants for a march into Eritrea in what threatened to turn into a religious war against the largely Muslim rebels. Although the invasion was called off, the fact that it was even envisioned shows how grave the Ethiopia-Eritrea dispute is.

These two developments could not offer clearer testimony to the timeliness of this study, also entitled *War Clouds on the Horn of Africa*. The research for it was done under the auspices of the Carnegie Endowment's International Fact-Finding Center which provides an opportunity for foreign affairs professionals to undertake anticipatory research on pre-crisis issues which carry significant threats to peaceful international relations. Even in mid-1974, as the center got under way, the Horn of Africa seemed to us to be a prototype pre-crisis situation full of potential conflict. Haile Selassie was an old man whose advanced age posed a major succession problem for his brittle regime. The leader of Kenya was equally advanced in years. The opening of the Suez Canal was soon to take place. The French presence in Djibouti was certain to undergo change. The rebellion in Eritrea continued to flare. Great-power interest in the area was increasing. The Endowment therefore asked Tom J. Farer, who had studied the politics and society of the Horn for many years, to undertake the necessary anticipatory research. This book is the result and from its pages several fundamental points emerge.

First, all the elements for serious international conflict are present: deep historical animosities, sharp national grievances, pressing economic problems, mischievous outside involvement. Also present are the sparks which any day could ignite major conflict, one which could begin locally but which, like an Angola — perhaps especially after Angola — could also draw in outside powers. This time, because of the proximity of the Suez Canal, the Persian Gulf, and the explosive Middle East, the interested outside powers may be less inclined to desist than at least one of them was in Angola. In this respect, the pending crisis on the Horn could represent — like the growing racial conflict in southern Africa — a serious threat to international peace and security.

Second, a crisis on the Horn could be perceived as another test for Soviet-American détente. Such tests should come on primary issues, but, in fact, they seem to be coming on secondary issues. If the superpowers cannot exercise some restraint as they deal with these less important questions, the concept of détente, as well as the phrase, will suffer further erosion. The issues on the Horn of Africa are so framed that if a conflict develops, either superpower can easily reach the conclusion that the other is exploiting détente to stake out new positions for itself outside its normal sphere of interest. The fragile character of détente gives the Horn an importance beyond the direct geographical or political stakes involved.

Third, the study shows that the prospects for peaceful settlement on the Horn are grim indeed without a cooperative approach to the region's problems by interested outside powers. The governments in the region, left to themselves and coping with the effects of outside involvement , have too few incentives to compromise. Yet the outside powers themselves will not provide these incentives so long as they view the pending crisis on the Horn as an opportunity to establish a position of enhanced influence or military presence rather than as a threat to their overall relationship.

Now in the summer of 1976, events and policies continue to drift. One may hope that Professor Farer's analysis will encourage governments in the region and outside powers alike to rethink policies which now are merely increasing the present level of misery and the future level of danger in the area.

As always, Endowment publication of this report implies a belief only in the importance of the subject. The views expressed are those of the author.

Comments or inquiries on this and other work of the Endowment may be addressed to the offices of the Carnegie Endowment for International Peace, 345 East 46th Street, New York, New York 10017 or 11 Dupont Circle, Washington, D.C. 20036.

Thomas L. Hughes
President
Carnegie Endowment for
International Peace

Acknowledgement

The "Acknowledgement" has been largely reduced to dehydrated ritual. But there being no other way publicly to express a real sense of gratitude, the form becomes as inevitable as the effort to transcend it.

Aside from its tendency to trivialize appreciation, the acknowledgement is irremediably invidious. During his famous libel suit against a critic who had imputed derisory value to his work, Whistler was asked on cross-examination how much actual time was required to complete one painting. Whistler responded unhesitatingly: "A lifetime!" So it is even in the less exalted realm of the modest technical study. Choosing a subject, weighing evidence, appraising behavior: All are governed decisively by the sum of everything the author has done and, in consequence, become, and of everyone he has known along the way. The only really satisfactory acknowledgement is, therefore, autobiography.

Since neither the Endowment nor the incipient crisis on the Horn can indulge the autobiographical instinct, I can enumerate only those who have contributed immediately to the completion of this venture. Needless to say, my gratitude to them is in no way diminished by my sense of a temporally wider network of support.

From the outset, I have enjoyed the unswerving encouragement, penetrating critique, and wry wit of Bill Maynes, director of International Programs for the Endowment. Margaret Cataldo, administrative assistant for the Fact-Finding Center, also has lent her generous support from the project's conception to its final, straining parturition. For being a lifeline to New York when I was in the field, an indefatigable compiler of current facts that might threaten fine-spun theories, and, above all, just for being herself, I am deeply in her debt. My debt is no less to Diane Bendahmane, my editor, who, together with the insoucient Maynes, managed, among other things, to restrain my more flatulent rhetorical flights. Nor, on the editorial side, can one overlook that sometimes laconic *eminence grise,* Endowment President Tom Hughes, who helped galvanize a major revision of one chapter with the elaborate annotation: "lightweight."

To be rewarded with an accurate typist may, in itself, exceed one's just desserts. When a typist also restores sanity to your spelling, operates successfully on your mangled syntax, and closes gaps in your research, you are hopelessly spoiled. Susan Fisher spoiled me and I am glad.

Many other members of the Endowment staff contributed to the pleasurable conclusion of this study. In particular I want to record my fond appreciation for the efforts of Rich Ferguson, Peggy Hanson, Betsey Brown, and Marguerite Jenkins. That feeling of appreciation also embraces my research assistant at Rutgers Law School, Jim Duffer, who demonstrated Herculean powers in bringing order out of the chaos of my field notes.

* * *

Considerations of confidentiality and, in a few cases, the sheer personal safety of my informants, preclude mentioning all who significantly helped me in grasping the complexities of political and military developments on the Horn itself and in the far larger region to which it relates geopolitically.

When I was in Addis Ababa, Ian Murray and Carl-Erhard Lindahl, respectively of the British and Swedish Embassies, offered warm hospitality and invaluable assistance. David Ottaway, the distinguished correspondent of the *Washington Post,* also helped light the way through the Ethiopian labyrinth. Members of the United States embassy, AID and MAAG officials were often helpful. To be sure, there were important differences of degree; but I prefer not to punctuate them.

Since the Horn is implicated in the affairs of the Middle East, my research led me to Israel and Lebanon. In both countries I was the beneficiary of generous hospitality and candid assessments. My resulting debts are too numerous to enumerate in full detail. However, I want particularly to express gratitude to my old and dear friend, Edward Said, my host and guide in Beirut. In Israel, Gideon Margalit opened doors it would have taken considerable time for me even to find, and Mordechai Abir, Israel's leading authority on the Horn, made me the rich beneficiary of his formidable knowledge and experience. I suspect that Mocca will not agree with all of my conclusions; I hope he will nevertheless feel that I have at least seen the relevant issues. Our dialogue will continue and will always be a great source of pleasure to me.

The mind of Pierre Mayer, special assistant to Michel Joubert during Joubert's tenure as French foreign minister, illuminates any topic it touches. His interests being catholic, the number of topics touched is vast. Fortunately for me, the Horn of Africa and the Persian Gulf were among them. He heightened my appreciation of issues that might otherwise have been obscure.

In the field of naval strategy, the autodidact is always threatening to trip and fall heavily. If, after this book has been perused by the professionals, I am merely limping as opposed to being immobilized with broken limbs, a very large part of the credit for mitigating damage should go to Commander James Patton, a member of the policy planning staff in the State Department. Like Abir and Mayer, he may be bemused by some of my conclusions; I hope that he will at least conclude that I raise the right issues, that I have not been unduly unfair to competing perspectives, and that the supporting analysis evidences my exposure to one of the few men in Washington's public or private life for whom the label "strategist" can rightly be taken as a sincere compliment.

Given the present volatility of political life on the Horn, description becomes an exercise not markedly different from efforts to nail mercury to the floor. Ann Reid of the State Department's Bureau of Intelligence and Research has read various parts of the manuscripts and has assisted my puffing attempt to remain current. She has also attempted, perhaps not always successfully, to straighten out apparently contorted pieces of analysis.

Over the years I have been privileged to have Colin Legum, commonwealth affairs editor of the *Observer,* as a friend and tutor. His vast knowledge of and penetrating insight into events on the African continent have been of inestimable value to me. I salute him for what he continues to be: a wise and compassionate man of iron integrity. I hope he finds merit in a book necessarily informed by an association I deeply value.

No acknowledgement would be complete without reference to my companion in the field, Jack Shepherd, who, by writing *The Politics of Starvation,* has added a new dimension of moral sensitivity to international disaster relief operations. The public is indebted to Jack as a supremely gifted journalist. But I am indebted to him as the friend who helped preserve sanity in the many airports where we awaited planes that hesitated to arrive and who was Africa's most dependable source of Lomatil. I am ready to go out with him again in search of a new crisis.

Tom J. Farer

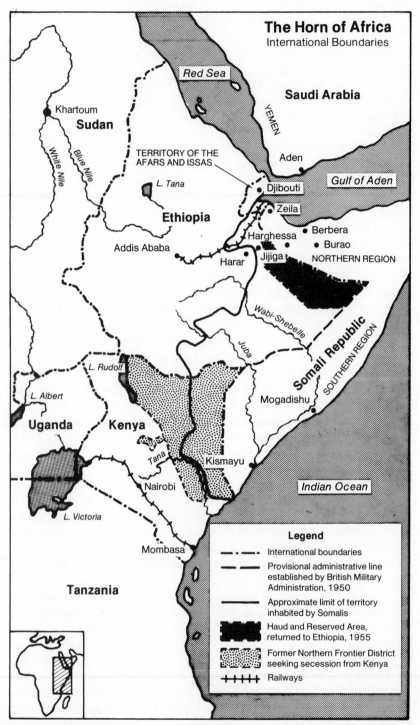

The Horn of Africa
International Boundaries

Red Sea

Saudi Arabia

YEMEN

Khartoum

Sudan

Aden

Gulf of Aden

TERRITORY OF THE
AFARS AND ISSAS

White Nile

Blue Nile

L. Tana

Djibouti

Zeila

Ethiopia

Harghessa

Berbera

Burao

Addis Ababa

Harar

Jijiga

NORTHERN REGION

Wabi-Shebelle

Somali Republic

SOUTHERN REGION

Juba

L. Rudolf

L. Albert

Mogadishu

Uganda

Kenya

Tana

Kismayu

Nairobi

Indian Ocean

L. Victoria

Legend

Mombasa

	International boundaries
	Provisional administrative line established by British Military Administration, 1950
	Approximate limit of territory inhabited by Somalis
	Haud and Reserved Area, returned to Ethiopia, 1955
	Former Northern Frontier District seeking secession from Kenya
	Railways

Tanzania

© John Drysdale. *The Somali Dispute* (New York: Praeger, 1964). Reprinted by permission of the publisher.

Introduction

Sir, to enable us to determine . . . with a firm and precise judgment, I think it may be necessary to consider distinctly the true nature and the peculiar circumstances of the object which we have before us. . . . I shall therefore endeavor, with your leave, to lay before you some of the most material of these circumstances in as full and as clear a manner as I am able to state them.

Edmund Burke. From a speech on moving resolutions for conciliation with the Colonies.

The Horn of Africa is roughly three-quarters of a million square miles in the northeast of the continent, consisting largely of eroding, ravine-slashed plateaus, seared bushland, and rubble-strewn volcanic desert. Being a metaphor rather than a political entity, it has no precise boundaries; but it is conventionally thought of as embracing Ethiopia, the Somali Democratic Republic, and the Territory of the Afars and the Issas, a French-controlled wedge between the Eritrean and Somali coasts often referred to by the name of its capital, only city, and port: Djibouti. The life of the vast bulk of its people is nasty, brutish, and short. An acute famine, which began in 1972 and killed at least 100,000 people and possibly several times that number,[1] has obscured the chronic decimation by disease and malnutrition.

In the northern province of Eritrea, Ethiopia's outlet to the Red Sea, the land is bled by a brutal secessionist struggle. My Lais follow Guernicas in a random and revolting procession. An ever-potential war between Somalia and Ethiopia will simply add to the agony of a population which presses remorselessly on the area's exiguous resources. And merely the risk of war complicates the task of ameliorating poverty and famine, a task to which the

1

revolutionary governments of both Ethiopia and the Somali Democratic Republic have formally consecrated themselves.

The present and potential destruction of human values on the Horn would be reason enough for international concern, even if the area's travail could be isolated. But, in fact, isolation is problematical since the potential belligerents touch the larger international system at many sensitive points.

In the first place, there is the elementary matter of geography. Clinging to the northeast edge of the African continent, both Ethiopia and Somalia seem implicated in the geopolitics of the Middle East and the whole northwest quadrant of the Indian Ocean including, of course, the Persian Gulf.

Israel's vital oil imports from Iran, as well as the renewing stream of Suez-bound commerce from the Gulf, East Africa, and Asia, must pass near the Somali coast, maneuver through the narrow Strait of Bab el Mandeb within a few miles of Africa, then debouch into the Red Sea and parallel the Ethiopian coast for 600 miles en route to the Strait of Tiran and the now tranquil Gulf of Aqaba. The Strait of Bab el Mandeb appears to some strategists as the point of maximum vulnerability. Today its African shore is part of that quaint remnant of France's colonial empire, the Territory of the Afars and the Issas. It is also one of the three chunks of foreign territory which, because of their large Somali-speaking populations, have been objects of Somalia's irredentist claims.

Geography is the force which has evoked varying degrees of superpower concern with the Horn. Under the terms of a mutual defense agreement signed in 1953, the United States has supplied Ethiopia with approximately $200 million worth of military assistance, virtually one-half of all U.S. military aid to sub-Sahara Africa during the past twenty-two years. The Ethiopian armed forces fly U.S. planes, fire U.S. rifles loaded with U.S. ammunition, and roll on U.S. tanks and trucks. Most of the officer corps has gone through U.S. training programs. Dependence on the United States for spare parts is virtually total. In 1975, with much-reduced support levels reflecting a sharp slackening of U.S. interest, the U.S. Military Assistance Advisory Group (MAAG) based in Addis Ababa still numbered more than fifty men, roughly one-half of the MAAG personnel in all of Africa.

The tie between the Somali Democratic Republic and the Soviet armed forces, initiated by a 1963 assistance agreement, is equally close. In 1963, the Somali army was a rag-tag affair consisting of some 5,000 ill-trained men carrying World War I-vintage rifles, without significant armor, and supported by a handful of moth-eaten planes superannuated out of the British and Egyptian air forces. According to the International Institute of Strategic Studies' respected survey of contemporary armed forces, by 1975 Somalia deployed approximately 23,000 men, 250 tanks and over 300 armored personnel carriers, and, by African standards, a respectably modern little air force. In armor and air power it compares favorably on paper with Ethiopia's military establishment. The net result is that, while in 1963 Ethiopia could have responded to Somali-inspired insurgency by marching to the sea, today U.S. military experts concede to the Somalis the capacity not only for effective defensive operations but also for an offense which could penetrate deeply into the contested border areas of Ethiopia before losing its momentum.

Even more than in the case of Ethiopia, Somali military capability is dependent on external support. The country's gross national product of $260 million is roughly one-tenth the size of Ethiopia's. It runs a permanent trade deficit, attracts trivial foreign investment, and has a currency virtually unrecognized outside the country's precincts.

In return for its not insubstantial services, the Soviet Union has been rewarded with most of the substance, though apparently not all the forms, of base rights. The principal Soviet installation is at the port of Berbera, by supersonic aircraft an instant's distance from Bab el Mandeb. According to Western intelligence experts—largely confirmed by participants in the Chaplinesque tour of Berbera arranged for U.S. congressional observers by the Somali government—the Soviets are still constructing a 12,000-foot airstrip, while having completed installations for moderate ship repairs, facilities for bunkering and ship-to-ship missile storage, and quarters for naval personnel, all protected by a SAM (surface-to-air missile) defense system. Certain areas of the port are under exclusive Soviet control. West of Berbera, near the small city of Harghessa, Soviet aircraft have access to a fighter base. Still a third airfield reportedly is under construction in the southern part of the country.

The ability to use the coastal areas and ports for the conduct of military operations against Red Sea or Indian Ocean commerce—and conversely, the ability to deny their use to antagonists—is persistently equated by certain strategists and their journalistic allies with "dominance" of the Red Sea trade route. For example, the *New York Times* has declared editorially that "an independent Eritrea functioning as an Arab satellite would not only deprive Ethiopia of its coastline but virtually turn the Red Sea into an Arab lake with potentially momentous consequences."[2] In a similar vein, C. L. Sulzberger has claimed that "through Somalia and the People's Democratic Republic of Yemen, Moscow now *controls* the southern approaches to the Red Sea and Suez."[3] Other analysts have gone further, announcing a risk of imminent Soviet domination of the whole Indian Ocean area and a consequent threat to fundamental Western interests.

Should we take these forebodings seriously? What are the real strategic implications of developments on the Horn? Can indigenous conflicts significantly affect the interests of other states? Can states external to the region moderate or aggravate the Horn's rooted conflicts? Rational answers to these questions presuppose not only a broad strategic vision but also an appreciation of the history, character, resources, and aspirations of the local actors in this contemporary drama of poverty, conflict and hope.

Notes

1. See Jack Shepherd, *The Politics of Starvation* (New York: Carnegie Endowment for International Peace, 1975) for the story of the drought and the cover-up which aggravated its deadly consequences.

2. *New York Times,* February 10, 1975.

3. *New York Times,* March 26, 1975. For other examples see Mordechai Abir, "Red Sea Politics" in *Conflicts in Africa. Adelphi Papers Number Ninety-three* (London: The International Institute for Strategic Studies, 1972), pp. 25-6; see also Abir, "The Reopening of the Suez Canal — Strategic Aspects," *Israel Defense Army Quarterly,* May 19, 1974; V. Matthies, "The Horn of Africa and International Relations," *Intereconomics* 12 (1974) : 385-7; *Newsweek,* November 12, 1974, p. 14; *Time,* January 4, 1971, p. 41; T. B. Millar, *The Indian and Pacific Oceans: Some Strategic Considerations. Adelphi Papers Number Fifty-seven* (London: The International Institute for Strategic Studies, 1969), pp. 4-6; *U.S. News and World Report,* January 24, 1972, pp. 32-4; Richard Schroeder, "Indian Ocean Policy," *Editorial Research Reports No. 10,* March 10, 1971, p. 204.

Part One

Ethiopia and Eritrea

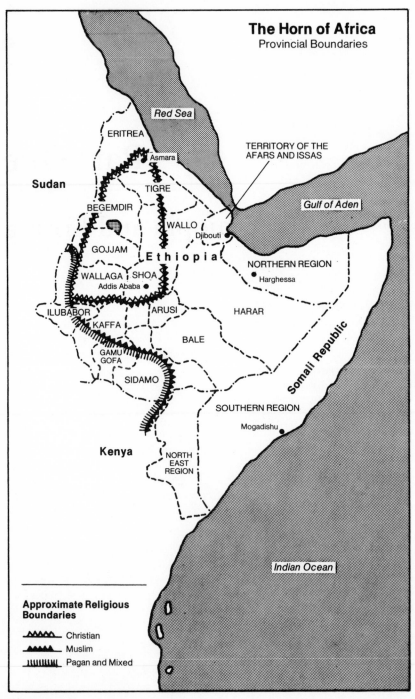

The Horn of Africa
Provincial Boundaries

Red Sea

ERITREA

Asmara

TERRITORY OF THE
AFARS AND ISSAS

Sudan

TIGRE

Gulf of Aden

BEGEMDIR

WALLO

Djibouti

GOJJAM

E t h i o p i a

NORTHERN REGION

Harghessa

WALLAGA | SHOA

Addis Ababa

ILUBABOR

ARUSI

HARAR

KAFFA

BALE

Somali Republic

GAMU
GOFA

SIDAMO

SOUTHERN REGION

Mogadishu

Kenya

NORTH
EAST
REGION

Indian Ocean

**Approximate Religious
Boundaries**

⚊⚊⚊⚊⚊ Christian

▲▲▲▲ Muslim

⊥⊥⊥⊥⊥⊥ Pagan and Mixed

© *Conflicts in Africa. Adelphi Papers Number Ninety-three.* (London: The International Institute for Strategic Studies, 1972). Reprinted by permission of the publisher.

Ethiopia 1

The Setting

Both geographically and politically, Ethiopia is dominated by a vast, thickly populated central highland, most of which is 6,000 to 8,000 feet above sea level. Frequent reference to the Ethiopian "tableland" obscures the real nature of the terrain which is carved up by canyons and gorges thousands of feet deep. The net effect is captured in a remark attributed to one member of the 1867 British Expeditionary Force: "They tell us this is a tableland. If it is, they have turned the table upside down and we are scrambling up and down the legs."

The reality, then, is a network of plateaus varying enormously in size and degree of isolation. Some are almost inaccessible. The terrain alone could explain why effective central rule has been exceptional in the course of Ethiopian history.

In the northwest, the plateau folds down into undulating grasslands which extend over the Sudanese border. On the east, opposite the northern part of the Somali Democratic Republic, it falls, often precipitously, into the Great Rift Valley before rising again as the Somali Plateau and making its way over to the sea. As the Rift Valley pushes north where it will finally be transformed into the Red Sea, it expands progressively and incorporates at its center one of the world's harshest deserts, the Danakil Depression, a blistering, rubble-strewn wasteland where the temperature can reach 140 degrees Fahrenheit and there is no shade. To the south and southeast, the highlands drop down into poorly watered bush country which presses deep into Kenya and the southern section of Somalia. And in the southwest, the plateau gives way to tropical forests from whose rich agricultural potential the curse of malaria is gradually being lifted.

Because of the altitude of its political heartland and also because of its historic remoteness, Ethiopia has often been compared to Switzerland or Tibet. During the just-concluded reign of Haile Selassie, however, the politically most revealing analogy is to Peter the Great's Russia. The main features are remarkably similar: an ethnic mosaic ruled by a rigidly centralized monarchy; the monarch's legitimacy resting on an ancient tradition and a national church; and the monarch himself surrounded by a horde of more-or-less dependent nobles and docile bureaucrats, supported by a large army, and committed only to that degree of modernization which would enhance his power and dignity. In Haile Selassie's case the degree was not very great, since the twentieth-century brand of modernization could not be harnessed to the purposes of an ancient monarchal order.

In both Peter's Russia and Selassie's Ethiopia, the ethnic group with which the monarch was identified to some degree dominated the institutions of the state, but other groups were by no means unrepresented. And just as the highest stratum of the favored group shared room at the top, its masses participated in the general misery at the bottom.

The depth of Ethiopian misery is pretty much invulnerable to exaggeration. By virtually any measure of social welfare or economic development, Ethiopia is one of the world's poorest countries. Its per capita gross national product is somewhere in the vicinity of $90, which places it among the bottom twenty nation-states. It is one of the eight states with an average per capita daily caloric intake of less than 1,600. Literacy is estimated at five percent of the population in contrast, for example, to the neighboring state of Kenya, where between twenty and twenty-five percent of the population is literate. Its transportation network is so exiguous that the average peasant must walk eight hours in order to reach a road on which wheeled vehicles of any kind can move. That is one, but only one, reason why tens of thousands can die of starvation while their government exports grain.

Among the diverse peoples who now cluster within the frontiers of Ethiopia, three — the Amharas, the Tigres, and the Gallas — have played the leading historic roles. The former two are Semitic in origin; speak related languages; live, respectively, in the central and northern highlands; and, with very few exceptions, are Coptic Christians. The Gallas, a Hamitic people who once preponderated along the Somali coast, pushed into the highlands during the sixteenth and seventeenth centuries. Although they arrived as a hostile force, they seem to have been domesticated rather rapidly. Substantial numbers converted to Christianity. Galla chiefs and Amhara nobles intermarried. In the twentieth century, there are Galla soldiers, bureaucrats, and landholders, and Galla blood runs in the veins of many noble Christian families.

The process of assimilation proceeded with sufficient speed so that, from the eighteenth century onward, regional and provincial rather than ethnic rivalries appear to have predominated in Ethiopian politics. For all that, the process of assimilation has never been completed, in part perhaps because many Gallas embrace Islam, in part perhaps because there are areas where Galla peasants have seen their interests in land subordinated to Christian aristocrats and soldiers who were the beneficiaries of imperial patronage. The historian Richard Greenfield describes a trip taken in 1958 to a large area under military administration "because a police column had been annihilated there in the mid-1950s."

> The writer journeyed around that region . . . with a military escort. . . . The *mulu asir-alika* (Sergeant) of the escort displayed almost 'colonialist' attitudes and boasted, 'The Galla are Amhara's slaves — they do as they are told,' and he also remarked, 'Their old men say that where Amhara comes the grass does not grow.' In some areas of Wellegga, also, local people are liable to despise 'Amhara' — who may well be Shewan Gallas — and may even refuse them water until they get to know them.

"But," Greenfield concludes, "these are largely peasant attitudes and prejudices not unlike those to be found in many ancient countries. They are fading and differ from the attitudes of the educated and of the future. . . ."[1] Perhaps; yet at least once during the 1960s, the Emperor found it necessary to stamp on a senior establishment figure of Galla ancestry who championed the rights of the Galla peasantry. The ethnic distinction may be dying, but it seems likely that an obituary is premature.

In the course of Ethiopian history, the locus of any effectively centralized power had often been in the Tigre-dominated portion of the realm. But at the end of the nineteenth century, the title of King of Kings passed to Menelik II, an Amharic-speaking claimant from the central highlands province of Shoa. And in Shoa it remained until September, 1974, when the Lion of Judah was bundled into a police Volkswagen and hauled off to enforced seclusion. Though suppressed during Haile Selassie's long reign, the traditional rivalry between the provinces of Shoa and Tigre may be a latent force for dissolution which could be activated by fragmentation of the military government which has succeeded Haile Selassie.

The Present as History

Without some modest grip on the paramount themes of Ethiopia's past, one is likely to encounter the present and future as impenetrable riddles. But in its gorgeous diversity, that past tends to elude any facile summary. With its court intrigues and fraternal strife, its tales of torture, betrayal, and murder, there is material for a thousand Jacobean dramas. There is also the stuff of epic poetry: the rise and fall of great kings and intervening dark ages of chaos, foreign invasions generating heroic wars of national defense, triumphs inevitably succeeded by decay in which the seeds of new triumphs eventually germinate. And through it all a culture—a vital though jagged sense of common identity—surviving over two millennia, resisting or assimilating invaders, comes at last, perhaps, to its rendezvous with the dissolving forces of modernization.

History shapes the present in part through the collective memory of its heirs. Today, as in the past, the Ethiopian elite is Christian. To be a Christian is to be a vicarious participant in thirteen centuries of intermittent conflict with the Islamic world. By A.D. 1000, the energies released by Mohammed's evangelism had catapulted Arabs across the Red Sea to wrench the African coast from Christian hands. In the subsequent centuries, the political frontier between Islam and Ethiopia has rolled back and forth in response to the shifting fortunes of war.

During the third decade of the sixteenth century, Ethiopian culture came close to the breaking point when the almost legendary Imam Ahmed Ibn Ibrahim Al-Ghazi, or Ahmed Gran ("The Left-Handed") as the Ethiopians called him, came storming up from the Somali coast in a *jihad* ("crusade") which marked its passage by pillaged towns, burned churches, and new converts for Islam. In ten years of unremitting conflict, his ethnically mixed force—including a large contingent of Somalis and stiffened in one crucial battle by 900 Arab, Turkish, and Albanian mercenary musketeers—poured over the central highlands and streamed north into Christianity's Tigrean redoubt.

With the help of some 400 Portuguese musketeers sent in response to desperate appeals for aid, the Ethiopians gradually turned the tide. In 1542, during what proved to be the decisive battle, Gran was killed and his army forced to retreat. Although for some years the struggle continued spasmodically, Islam as an armed force gradually receded, leaving in its wake, however, a large though politically impotent body of believers.

Gran's *jihad* was the high-water mark but not the end of the Islamic threat. Even three centuries later, long after Islam's eclipse as a dynamic force in international politics, a morally regenerative eruption on its African periphery, the Mahdists* of the Sudan, was able to threaten Ethiopian national existence. And again at the cost of a dismembered emperor,** the lords of the nation and their teeming followers streamed out to meet and break the Islamic lance.

To this day, it is commonplace for educated Ethiopians to remark: "We are a Christian island in an Islamic sea." This rooted perception of an irremedial enmity can hardly facilitate amicable resolution of the Eritrean insurgency, which is sustained by Arab arms as well as by just grievances, or the confrontation with the Somali Democratic Republic, a nation of devout Muslims and a member of the Arab League.

A second feature of Ethiopian history which shadows the present is the tenuous nature of central authority. The Emperor's title, King of Kings, was not grandiloquence; it was literal, historic truth. There were many provincial dynasties; only occasionally did one succeed in coordinating all or most of the others. During his half-century reign, Haile Selassie faced and repeatedly crushed regionally-based challengers. Despite Selassie's efforts to extend the nerves of government into every region of the national body, the difficult terrain, the lilliputian road work, the shrunken educational system, the immensity of the land, the torpor of the government's bureaucracy, and the persistence of ethnic diversity all have conspired to limit the penetration of central authority and to sustain a centrifugal potential. Fearful of that potential, any central government, whether radical or conservative in its social policies, is likely — out of fear of the precedent's contagion — to resist demands for real regional autonomy, much less independence.

A third feature of Ethiopian history with contemporary resonance is the repeated use of the East African coast, par-

---

*The Mahdists were the followers of a messianic religious leader (a Mahdi) named Mohammed Ahmed, who wrested Khartoum from General Charles George ("Chinese") Gordon and thereafter, until his defeat by Anglo-Egyptian forces under General Horatio Kitchener, dominated the Sudan.

**During the continuing struggle following Gran's death, Muslim forces killed the Ethiopian emperor Gahados and delivered his head to one of Gran's widows.

ticularly along the Red Sea, as a point of departure for
Ethiopia's enemies when they invaded the Christian heartland. In
1868, Massawa was the port of disembarkation for Field Marshal
Sir Robert Napier's extravagant force, complete with elephants
and a brass band, which paraded into the highlands to release
the British consul and a handful of other Europeans imprisoned
by Emperor Tewodros, Ethiopia's version of Ivan the Terrible.[2]
Napier's departure coincided with the revival of Egyptian power.
Influenced, Greenfield suggests, by the suddenly enhanced
significance of the Red Sea following the opening of the Suez
Canal, Egypt seized control of the sea's entire western coast. By
1875, Egyptian troops were pressing on the Ethiopian highlands
all along its curving periphery. But within a year, they were virtually annihilated by an Ethiopian army under the command of
Emperor Yohannes IV. Egypt retained only a precarious toe-hold
on the Red Sea coast. And even that was relinquished a few years
later when the Mahdists raised the standard of rebellion against
the Egyptians in the Sudan.

The Italians were next. Belated initiates of the Imperial
Club, by the mid-1880s they had hacked out a 50,000-square-
mile triangle with its apex in the Tigrean highlands. They called
it Eritrea. During this first stage, progress was eased by a de facto
alliance with Emperor Menelik II, who needed Italian weapons
to consolidate his fissiparous empire. The alliance quickly shattered when it became apparent that the Italians regarded Eritrea
merely as an hors d'oeuvre. Having no intention of constituting
an entrée, Menelik moved decisively against his erstwhile Christian allies when they came knifing out of the Eritrean salient.
The coming disaster was veiled by a series of inconclusive skirmishes with elements of the numerically superior forces rallying
to Menelik from every part of the country. Finally, at Adowa in
1896, the Ethiopians fell en masse on the Italian army and tore it
to shreds.

Four decades later, the Italians came back, this time with
planes, poison gas, and a larger army, under Rodolfo Graziani,
fleshed out with African units recruited in Eritrea and Somalia.
While the Emperor retired, despite the vigorous opposition of
some of his supporters, to plead Ethiopia's case abroad and to
plot his return, guerrilla groups sprang up all over the country,
first to bleed the occupying force and later to assist in its demoli-
tion by a British contingent one-tenth its size. Six years after the
invasion, the Italians were prisoners in what they had conceived
of as the fulcrum of their East African empire.

From Gran to Graziani, the record is constant: sooner or

later the highlands expel foreign objects. The achievement has bred self-confidence; but its price, so frequently paid during the past century, can hardly encourage initiatives which would reduce Ethiopian control over the Red Sea coast.

After the Fall of the Lion

Revolutionary forces had been accumulating for years behind the dam of the Emperor's hardening opposition to change. Journalists, historians, and diplomats dutifully recorded the rising level of frustration, but few if any imagined that it might overwhelm the Lion of Judah, much less two thousand years of monarchal and theocratic government. Like his long-lived Spanish contemporary, Haile Selassie had spun around himself an aureole of invulnerability. It is doubtful that even the prospective agents of revolution imagined that their time would come round until the Emperor demonstrated that he was in fact mortal.

Events beyond the reach of this diminutive political genius conspired against a grand Wagnerian exit. The acute rise in the price of oil fueled inflationary pressures in the cities and traumatized the small but critically positioned middle class of industrial workers, civil servants, and soldiers. Meanwhile, in parts of the highlands, above all in the provinces of Wallo and Tigre, a murderous drought consumed the countryside.

From 1970 through 1972, almost no rain had fallen. With their plow oxen dead or dying, their seed grain largely consumed for food, their own bodies pathetically weakened, the peasants were powerless to exploit the long rains of 1973. The harvest was derisory. Having lost everything, those who could still move began to trek out of the countryside in search of help. Thousands of skeletal corpses marked their passage. Gradually, an army of scarecrows collected in the towns and cities or clotted along the few roads, halting with their bodies trucks bound for the coast with grain and vegetables for export.

As early as November, 1972, the first word of the disaster was trickling into the capital's torpid bureaucracy. The annual crop survey circulated that month by the Ministry of Agriculture accurately detailed the areas of crop failure and forecast "widespread food shortages."[3] The Council of Ministers responded early the following year by ordering the minister of agriculture to suppress the survey. That was the beginning of an official coverup, a conspiracy of silence that would implicate within twelve months every foreign embassy and bilateral and multilateral aid mission in Addis Ababa.

The imperial Ethiopian government was prepared to admit that there was a problem. What it would not concede through the whole of 1973 and into the early months of 1974 was the dimension of the problem and its own plain inability to cope. As late as March, 1974, with perhaps 100,000 peasants already dead, the government labeled descriptions of the disaster then beginning to circulate freely in Europe as "wishful malice."[4]

The failure to act was a compound of arrogance, indifference, incompetence, and amour-propre — a compound, in short, of everything that was rotten in the state of Ethiopia. Drought and famine, some officials said privately, were immutably part of the cycle of existence in Ethiopia. From time to time, the rains failed. Peasants died. This had always been the case. It was nothing new. A major feeding program would set a dangerous precedent. Millions might become dependent on the government. And the government could not afford such largesse.

Above all, there was the question of "face." Ethiopia was not some crumbly little Sahelian country stamped out of French dough. It was a great and ancient empire with a history and culture to match that of any state. If it could not feed its own people, how could it claim equality of place in international councils?

And so while it was prepared to receive assistance, the imperial government, which in practice meant Haile Selassie, would not allow the aid and relief agencies to declare publicly the terrible need. As one minister put it, "If we can save the peasants only by confessing our failure to the world, it is better that they die."[5] Which they did.

Even without an accelerated international relief effort, many might have been saved if the government could only have organized its domestic resources. It essayed feeble gestures which served only to re-emphasize its ineffable corruption and incompetence. Money collected from civil servants ordered to tithe and from students who voluntarily abstained from breakfast simply disappeared.

Present failures were multiplied by past neglect. Wallo was the forgotten province. Its people had scorned the Emperor as an upstart. Retreating from the Italian armies in 1935, he had hastened through the province while its citizens gathered to spit upon him. The Emperor had a long memory. He had built few roads anywhere in the empire; but in Wallo there were virtually none at all, just as there were no hospitals, or schools, or any other earnest of imperial concern. So food could not be brought into the villages, and the villagers could not reach the feeding centers until, in tens of thousands of cases, it was too late.

Famine relief was not the only governmental function infected with incompetence and corruption. The infection was equally rampant in the army's supply system. And its ultimate victims were not peasants conditioned to stoic docility by history, the Emperor, and the church, but rather armed men who even in the lower ranks had, by virtue of their training, been in varying degrees detached from the traditional pieties. The main burden of corruption fell on common soldiers and their noncommissioned officers (NCOs). When a grain ration arrived mixed with sand to compensate for the amount diverted into commercial channels, they suffered. Maladministration aggravated the injury of meager salaries shrinking in the face of a suddenly galloping inflation. Discontent seems to have been particularly acute in the Second Division which had borne the brunt of the endless conflict in Eritrea.

In retrospect, it now seems clear that revolt was also simmering in the ranks of the younger officers. These were educated men. More than a few had studied abroad. All of them must have been sensitive to their country's acute underdevelopment relative to African states only recently released from colonialism. As soldiers and Ethiopians, they were ardent nationalists. But their ties to the existing order of things were relatively loose.

The armed forces were the most democratic institution in the empire. Officers were drawn from every part of the country and only rarely from the aristocracy. They manned not only the most democratic but also the most effective institution. For all its corruption, most of it at the top, the army *functioned*. It had fought not without valor in Korea and the Congo. It had held on in Eritrea and thrashed the Somalis in a brief but bloody border skirmish in 1974. Until the beginning of the 1970s, many observers had rated it the best army in black Africa with the possible exception of Nigeria.

But now the balance seemed to be shifting toward Somalia where, in 1969, the army had overthrown its own corrupt civilian government and installed a junta committed to national strength and revolutionary reform. By 1974, it had doubled the number of men at arms, equipped them with the largest armored force between the Sahara and South Africa, and coincidentally begun to effect a genuine social revolution. It is doubtful that Ethiopian officers failed to appreciate either the precedent or the contrast with their own flaccid government which could neither feed its people nor even attract any longer the guns and tanks and planes which had assured Ethiopian pre-eminence on the Horn.

In late February of 1974, the combustible elements in the

Ethiopian armed forces finally ignited. The flame of mutiny raced through the streets of Asmara. To this day, there are conflicting reports of who took the initiative in Asmara and subsequently in Addis and Harar among the three other divisions of the army, as well as the elite airborne unit and, finally, the air force. Some observers claim it was a revolt from the bottom, a mutiny of private soldiers and their sergeants. Others insist that the younger officers were deeply involved from the outset, though sometimes disguised as NCOs, so great was their initial fear of imperial retribution.

The locus of leadership was obscured, in part at least because of the apparent unanimity within the Second Division below the level of its general officers. Rejecting the authority of their commanders, the troops dispatched a series of demands to the Emperor. Wholly unrevolutionary in content, they sounded like nothing more than the manifesto of a soldier's trade union: a litany of better pay and higher fringe benefits. The government, carefully distinguished from His Imperial Majesty, was condemned for its failure to protect the interests of its men at arms.

In his response, the Emperor was equally careful to disclaim any threat to imperial authority. Alluding obliquely to fears that he might order mass punishments for the Second Division, he said that no one could condemn men who had simply exercised the right of all loyal subjects to petition their Emperor.

That was a nice gesture; but, even coupled with concessions on pay, it did not get the cork back into the bottle. Excitement and a kind of creative turmoil began rippling through all the units of the armed forces. Within days, the spark had leaped over to the organized civilian population, particularly in Addis. Workers struck, students marched, demands began to multiply and escalate.

Patently embarrassed by civilian condemnation of the parochial character of their demands and sensing, perhaps, that the dam really had begun to give way, the troops began to inject revolutionary political content into their manifestos. The government was condemned for corruption and the failure to alleviate the famine whose dimensions were now widely appreciated. And far more ominously, there came the demand for constitutional reform.

The Emperor remained an island of formal serenity amidst these oceanic emotions. If the politicians — all, of course, wholly his creatures, subordinate to imperial control in even their most minor acts — had failed, they had to be replaced. He accepted the resignation of Prime Minister Aklilu Habte-Wold and his colleagues who had presided over the coverup of the drought, then called on one of the cabinet members, Endalkachew Makonnen, to form a new government. An elegant, suave graduate of Oxford, linked to powerful aristocratic families, Endalkachew hardly mirrored the growing revolutionary spirit. Nevertheless he accepted the mandate, chose a cabinet, and with the Emperor's approval established a committee of experts to draft a new constitution.

Meanwhile, the Emperor maintained the elegant, stately ritual of his imperial rounds. But behind this facade of imperturbability, it is reported that he began the intricate, subtle maneuvers that had so often before preserved his position. No deep appreciation of the Ethiopian scene was required to detect deep rifts within the armed forces and between it and the civilian radicals, particularly the students. Haile Selassie had spent a lifetime balancing off against each other potential sources of opposition. The senior command structure was riven by personal, regional, and ethnic feuds. And there were few men of high position in the armed forces or the civil government who had not enjoyed forms of imperial favor which, being without legislative or other formal authorization, would in a modern government fall plainly under the rubric of "corruption." They were, therefore, sorely limited in their capacity to respond with enthusiasm to the crescendoing demands in the cantonments of the army, the university, and the streets to punish the corrupt. So even if the senior dignitaries of the empire had been playing an important role in the movement for reform, they could hardly have avoided trying to deflect it from any radical demarche. But, in fact, they were powerless.

By midspring, the armed forces — soldiers and officers acting as a single body — had elected representatives to an Armed Forces Coordinating Committee. No one above the rank of colonel was eligible; along with everyone else, generals could cast one vote for candidates. This limitation was necessary, the organizers said, for if senior officers served on the committee, either they would intimidate with their rank or they would lose their authority to command in the field. One hundred and twenty men were elected: sergeants, warrant officers, captains, majors from units scattered throughout the empire; anonymous men, and so they were called collectively the Dergue, the "shadow." And by slow and subtle degrees, they began to gnaw away the throne of the Lion of Judah.

The arrests, which by September would vacuum up virtually the entire senior elite that had served as the eyes, ears, and arms of the Emperor, began early in Endalkachew Makonnen's brief tenure. The arrivistes went first, men like the deposed prime minister, Aklilu Habte-Wold, who had risen on the strength of the Emperor's favor, often extended to those of modest background who demonstrated loyalty and ability in his service. Virtually all of Endalkachew's colleagues in the prior cabinet were soon ensconced in the rough barracks of the Addis-based Fourth Division. Charged with corruption and criminal negligence in the matter of the drought, they awaited promised investigations and trial.

In the meantime, the capital played host to such prodigies as a four-day general strike, probably the first successful effort of its kind in the short history of independent black Africa, and a demonstration by an estimated 30,000 Muslims demanding equal rights. Concessions tumbled from the new government: wage increases for teachers and the lowest-paid civil servants; appointment of a committee to investigate corruption in the previous government; new proposals for land reform, that perennial of official rhetoric. Throughout the country, the cauldron of long-suppressed grievances continued to boil. Tax collectors, provincial administrators (notorious for their lassitude and corruption), and, in some parts of the empire, landlords found life increasingly perilous. Particularly in the south where the Gallas had been incorporated by conquest and their lands assigned to Shoan officers in the Imperial Army, latent peasant antagonism bubbled violently to the surface.

Endalkachew's government could concede, but it seemed incapable of dramatic action. There was, after all, no tradition of ministerial initiative. Indeed, for decades nothing had been better calculated to assure departure from the political scene than a show of independent judgment. Constitutions and cabinets had come and gone, while the Emperor remained the brains and the heart of real government. Endalkachew and his colleagues, having risen in the old system, could hardly have been disposed psychologically to break loose from its constraints. Moreover, it was by no means clear, on the one hand, how far the Emperor wanted them to go in meeting the demands for reform and, on the other, whether effective power had slipped definitively from his hands. The overriding impression one had visiting Addis in the summer of 1974 was the paralyzing fear which suffused the civil government. Torpid under the best of circumstances, trained to passivity by the Emperor's carrots and sticks, it was totally incapable of responding to the cascade of demands which poured down upon it.

The Dergue rumbled its dissatisfaction with the pace of change. The pattern of arrests broadened. Judges, generals, provincial governors, and aristocrats were added to the guest list at the "Fourth Division Hilton." The Emperor's cadre of advisors and aids began to dwindle, although the daily ritual of consultation and supplication continued. Piece by piece, the Dergue was dismantling the *ancien régime.*

Not without internal tensions, to be sure. The worst threat to its cohesion arose early in the game, in March, when airborne troops swarmed over Debre Zeit Air Base, thirty miles from the capital, seized a covey of young officers, and locked up the ordnance. The action was justified by an alleged plot to bomb the Imperial Palace and precipitate Haile Selassie's removal, an allegation firmly denied by the air force which proceeded to sulk throughout the spring. One of the many rumors that slithered through the fevered city was that the real reason for the paratroopers' action was the corruption of their commanding officer by the Palace. Similar rumors of imperial funds being circulated discretely undoubtedly stiffened and spread the conviction that the Emperor would never consent to a graceful transition to constitutional impotence.

The future of the Emperor was one of the issues reckoned by the diplomatic and journalistic communities and the Addis rumor-mill to divide Dergue members. Some officers, it was believed, favored his formal removal coincident with transformation of the monarchy into a strictly ceremonial position. Others seemed intimidated by the widely held belief that any move against the Emperor would galvanize the mass of Ethiopians into armed resistance to the Dergue.

Uncertainty about the true strength of the old order undoubtedly braked the momentum of revolutionary change and encouraged the Dergue to lurk behind the increasingly hollow forms of monarchal and parliamentary government. Foreign journalists wrote ominously that the Ethiopian populace was the world's most heavily armed, that there were nine million guns in private hands, 300,000 in Addis alone, that you could purchase grenades and submachine guns in the market, that provincial aristocrats could mobilize well-armed private armies, and finally that, if threatened with the secularization of the state, the Coptic church could unleash this heavily armed mass of true believers, plunging the empire into a maelstrom of blood.

As spring gave way to summer, the suspicion began to spread

that the lions of the old order were, in fact, toothless. Day after day, their numbers were shrunk by arrests both in Addis and in their provincial strongholds. At the end of June, the constitutional experts brought forth a set of concrete proposals. Their draft provided for a constitutional monarchy with merely ceremonial functions, parliamentary rule, and a secular state. The Patriarch of the Ethiopian Orthodox church, Abune Teofilos,* denounced the proposal to transform religion into a matter of purely private conscience. But the capital remained quiet.

Frustrated by the paralysis of the civil government, emboldened by the passivity of the elite, and embittered by efforts to fracture their unity, the members of the Coordinating Committee began to move out from behind the scene.

In early August, they forced the resignation of Endalkachew's government, dispatched Endalkachew himself to the detention center, and appointed in his place an aristocrat, Michael Imru, who had for years languished in unwanted diplomatic sinecures because of his unambiguous commitment to serious reform. The new government was also distinguished by its minister of defense, Gen. Aman Michael Andom, a favorite of the armed forces both because of his martial virtues and his reputation for incorruptibility.

The change in government did not, however, generate any noticeable momentum in the pace of reform. The Dergue wanted instant change. No civilian government could produce it, or at least so it now appeared to the leaders of the revolution. And so on September 12, 1974, they moved to fill the vacuum of authority and to break decisively with the old order. They drove to the Palace where Haile Selassie, after fifty years at the apex of government, waited utterly alone, already stripped of every instrument of power. He looked, it is said, with some disdain at the little blue Volkswagen, then stepped into the back seat and was driven out through the Palace gates, where a small, hostile crowd hurled epithets at the tiny, bearded ascetic who had finally lost his struggle with history.

With him went the last civilian government. At the request of the Dergue, General Aman assumed the prime ministership, while retaining the defense portfolio. In addition, he was named chief of staff. He would, moreover, serve as the ceremonial head of state pending the return of the Crown Prince, who was invited to assume the office of constitutional monarch; and finally the general was designated chairman of the Provisional Military Ad-

---

*The Dergue arrested him in February, 1976.

ministrative council, that is, of the Dergue now transformed by its own will into the formal agency of executive and legislative power. Despite the general's several titles, including his chairmanship of the council, it was widely assumed that he remained an instrument rather than the leader of the revolutionary elite.

Having assumed the indicia as well as the substance of power, the new rulers of the ancient kingdom had at last to confront their differences. Several fundamental issues appeared to fracture opinion among these still largely anonymous men: Should there be a military or a civilian government? How should the old elite be treated? Should there be conciliation or more repression in Eritrea? How might government be decentralized? And what should be the character of land reform? Any one of these issues might have been the first to draw blood, mangling the quite extraordinary unity which the Dergue had maintained in the face of persistent efforts to play upon differences of ideology as well as of region, ethnicity, and rank. But if one had had to project the issue from which the first blood would gush, the choice would inevitably have fallen on Eritrea.

Notes

For information on the history and ethnology of Ethiopia, the author is particularly indebted to the works of Richard Greenfield, Donald N. Levine and Dame Margerie Perham: Greenfield, *Ethiopia: A New Political History* (New York: Praeger, 1965); Levine, *Wax and Gold* (Chicago: University of Chicago Press, 1965) and *Greater Ethiopia* (Chicago: University of Chicago Press, 1975); and Perham, *The Government of Ethiopia* (London: Faber & Faber, 1969). Also helpful was *Area Handbook for Ethiopia* (Washington, D.C.: American University Foreign Area Studies, 1971) by Kaplan, Faber *et al.*

1. Greenfield, p. 7.

2. For a brilliant account of this extravaganza, see Alan Moorehead, *The Blue Nile* (New York: Harper & Row, 1962), pp. 235-6.

3. Jack Shepherd, *The Politics of Starvation* (New York: Carnegie Endowment for International Peace, 1975), pp. 13-14.

4. Shepherd, p. 15.

5. *New York Times,* May 19, 1974.

2 Eritrea

The Making of a State

Eritrea is an accidental place, the remnant of Italian imperial dreams after the disaster of Adowa. Its two and one-half million people, forming an ethnic mosaic hardly less diverse than Ethiopia's, originally had nothing in common other than common domicile within a colony's arbitrary frontiers. The frontiers split several cultural communities, among which by far the largest were the Tigrinya-speaking* Christian Tigres of the northern highlands; roughly one-third were cut off in Eritrea from their brothers in the adjoining Ethiopian province of Tigre.

At the turn of the century, it must have seemed inevitable that the Tigre overlap, connecting more than a quarter of Eritrea's population to Ethiopia, would constitute a running sore on the body of Italian authority. In fact, during the colonial era, the Tigres proved no less tractable than other Christians or the Islamic segment of the

---

* Languages from both the Hamitic and Semitic families are spoken in Ethiopia, Gallinya, a Hamitic language of the Cushite group, is spoken in southern and northeastern Ethiopia and is related to Afar, Somali, and other languages spoken south of Ethiopia.

The relationship among the Semitic languages is somewhat complicated. In the north, there are Tigrinya and Tigre. These languages are spoken in Eritrea and in the Ethiopian province of Tigre. There, Tigrinya is the major language, Tigre being spoken by a relatively small number of people, all of them Muslims who live in the coastal plains and northern highlands of Eritrea. Although Tigre and Tigrinya are related languages, geographical barriers have long separated the Tigres so that their languages are now mutually unintelligible.

In the central area of Ethiopia they speak Amharic, the official language of the country. As French and Spanish spring from Latin, Amharic, Tigrinya and Tigre spring from a common root language (Geez) which survives only for certain ecclesiastical purposes.

native population. From the colony's founding until British occupation in 1941, Italy ruled unchallenged. It was even able to recruit Eritreans for service in the army which invaded Ethiopia in 1935.*

If the Italians did not provoke much open opposition to their rule, they did not build a large reservoir of affection either. Once Italian prestige was deflated by British victory, the "friendly" natives showed signs of a well-nourished hostility which was sharply intensified by gradually increasing head-to-head economic competition, in which the Eritreans did not fare well, and by the inauguration of Ethiopia's campaign to annex Eritrea as part of the postwar settlement.

With the fervent support of the Coptic church, the traditional bearer of Ethiopian nationalism whose clerical network covered the

---

*Success in avoiding internal opposition cannot be attributed to the peculiarly enlightened or liberal character of Italian rule for the simple reason that it was neither enlightened nor liberal. Like the British in Kenya, the Italians had come not merely to govern but to live. A thin stream of the Mezzogiorno's favorite export, people, was directed south away from the main current flowing to the Western Hemisphere. By the 1930s, the Italian element in a total population of perhaps one million had swollen to roughly 40,000.

Goaded by their unassuageable hunger for the best land, best jobs, and superior caste status, settlers inevitably demand crude discrimination against indigenous populations. The encouragement of immigration being a major purpose of colonial rule, the Italian administration, even before it was envenomed by fascism, was bound to sympathize with settler priorities. Discrimination assumed the familiar pattern of carefully limited educational opportunities, exclusion from middle and upper levels of the police, judicial, and administrative bureaucracies, preclusion of political activity, and denial of development-related goods and services.

Yet the population remained passive. Why? First, because fragmentation along the fault lines of race, religion, vocation, region, and clan left few openings for cooperation in pursuit of any purpose. Second, the Italian presence created relatively attractive economic opportunities for a substantial number of impoverished Eritreans, benefits which multiplied in the late 1920s and early 1930s when Italy began preparing the infrastructure of its East African empire. However menial, the jobs provided benefits in excess of very low pre-existing expectations. It would take some time for the base of economic aspirations to rise above that which the Italians were willing to concede. Third, the Italian administration did not attempt radical alteration of social and economic patterns in the countryside where most Eritreans lived. Fourth, the fact that the Italians were, after all, Christian and in that sense participants in the historic alliance against the Islamic world may have helped to allay the antagonism of the Tigres who, by virtue of their numbers, ties to Ethiopia, and relative preponderence in administrative jobs, were the most dangerous threat to the colony's tranquillity. Finally, it would be naive to overlook three strategic considerations: the large and growing army south of Suez maintained by the Italians with an eye to eventual expansion; the territory's modest size (50,000 square miles, only one-tenth the size of Ethiopia) ; and its accessibility through the two ports of Massawa and, further south, Assab.

Eritrean highlands, the Emperor fostered the growth of a unionist party which quickly became the dominant voice among Eritrean Christians. This party was, however, opposed at all times by a small minority of Christian separatists who recognized that the imperial impulse is not restricted to the white race. Initially favoring independence, following a massacre in August, 1946, of Christian Eritreans by Muslim soldiers from the Sudan Defense Force, the separatists effected a brief rapprochement with the unionists on the basis of joint support for an autonomous state within the framework of the Ethiopian empire. But rapprochement quickly shattered on the rock of Haile Selassie's distaste for a federal solution. The separatists thereupon reverted to their original position, festooned, however, with a claim for the "restoration" of Tigre Province to Eritrea, a development which would, of course, have had the, for them, happy consequence of guaranteeing a solid Christian majority in the new state.

The Muslim community, constituting about half the colony's population, reacted more slowly to the political opportunity created by Italy's defeat and her formal renunciation of all right and title to her colony. Its largest component, the Tegray tribes, ethnic cousins of the Christian Tigres, who spread from the tip of the predominantly Christian plateau to the western lowlands bordering the Sudan, was initially preoccupied with other matters. The attention of the lowland Tegrays was absorbed by a vicious little struggle between them and a tribe on the Sudanese side of the border. The highland Tegrays were convulsed by internal conflict: a threatened uprising of serfs, supported by merchants in the main north highland towns, against the traditional aristocratic families. During World War II the festering struggle of the serfs was restrained by an unstable British compromise. At the war's conclusion it intensified and spread to all Tegray tribes. Confronted, by the end of 1946, with a situation where nine-tenths of the Tegray population was united in opposition to the aristocratic remainder, the British administration committed itself to a process of emancipation.

The emancipation struggle raised political consciousness throughout the Muslim community and honed leaders able to give it effective expression. In December, 1946, Ibrahim Sultan Ali, a townsman who had become the most prominent figure in the emancipation movement, organized a meeting of representatives from all the Muslim groups to consider the question of Eritrea's future. The meeting produced an organization (the Muslim League with Ibrahim Sultan as secretary-general), a negative program (opposition to union with Ethiopia), and a bundle of disagreements over the alternatives to union. After a long wrangle, the various factions coalesced loosely around independence, either immediately or "in case this is held to be impossible, . . . an international trusteeship . . . for ten years . . . with British control or such control as may be directed by the Trusteeship Council of the U.N.O."[1]

The unionist cause was strengthened, inadvertently, by both British and Italian policy. From the outset, British occupation policy was laissez faire in conception. Faced with an enthusiastically Fascist settler community, the British, determined to maintain control with a minimum commitment of men and resources and eager to use the colony as an entrepôt and arsenal for their North African campaign, simulated the snail more than the hare in altering the structure of Italian ascendancy. Acrid land disputes between Eritreans and settlers continued to be litigated before Italian judges who applied Italian colonial law. Although the British displaced Italians at the apex of the administration, just below it Italian functionaries remained at their desks, and Eritrean clerks at their disposal. Incentives for enhanced agricultural production were generally awarded, in the name of superior efficiency, to Italian farmers. Concerned with winning the war, not with promoting in Eritrea greater levels of social justice than those obtaining in English colonies, the British administration actually appropriated some Eritrean-owned land and transferred it to Italian hands.

A division of the social and economic spoils which seemed tolerable — or at any rate was tolerated — when the Italians were at the top of the heap quickly became intolerable after they had fallen a notch and become, like the Indians in the British colonies of East Africa, a buffer between the administrative heights and the indigenous population. The emergent hostility was not limited to harsh glances and nasty words. Particularly in the countryside, a number of Italians were put to the knife. Hostility was compounded when settler hopes for the restoration of Italian rule or at least de facto hegemony began to rise. Kindled originally by the retention of economic ascendancy and British insistence on treating Eritrea as occupied *Italian* territory, hostility ignited as Italy belatedly switched rulers and sides, then flared when the cold war produced suitors from both East and West for the Italian hand.

The postwar atmosphere, although friendlier than Italy might justifiably have hoped at the time of its surrender, was clearly inimical to the restoration of full colonial rule over Somalia, Eritrea, and Libya. Trusteeships, on the other hand, seemed within reach. In Somalia, reach and grasp coincided rather neatly despite harsh indigenous opposition. But in Eritrea, the Italians had also to contend with the astute diplomacy of Haile Selassie, whose canonization in the democracies as an anti-Fascist hero obscured the tough authoritarian nature of his own political enterprise.

Quickly recognizing that restoration of colonial status was unattainable, the settlers, with Italian government support, pressed first for Italian trusteeship and then, when that too began to drift out of reach, for independence. They apparently assumed, not implausibly, that an independent Eritrea would look to Italy for economic assistance and also for political support against Ethiopian imperialism and would, moreover, allow the settlers to play a mediating role between the Muslim and Christian parties. The swing toward independence by the settlers and their local clients led to the formation of a strong independence bloc incorporating the Muslim League, the Liberal Progressive Party of Christian Separatists, and the settler-dominated organizations. With the aid of lavish Italian disbursements, the bloc began to eat away unionist support, including a corporal's guard of Muslim renegades.

The unionists responded with all the weapons at their disposal. Christian waverers were coerced by the church's threatened denial of access to the sacraments. Tegray tribesmen, who in the past had often roamed across the Ethiopian frontier in search of grazing during the dry months of winter and spring, suddenly found their way barred by the Ethiopian authorities unless they could produce Unionist party membership cards. For Christians or anyone else who supported independence, there was, finally, an ample supply of terror.

It had flared up before the bloc's formation in connection with a 1948 fact-finding visit by a commission representing the Big Four (France, Britain, the United States, and the USSR). Following a period of moderating violence, the bloc's formation and the prospective visit of a United Nations investigatory commission fueled a new wave of terror.

Between October 1949 and the arrival of the United Nations Commission in February 1950, 9 Italians, an Indian, a Greek, 3 Christian supporters of the Bloc, and 4 Moslem tribesmen were assassinated. Italian cafes in Asmara and Addi Ugri were attacked with rifle fire and hand-grenades; hand-grenades were thrown at Italian and Eritrean supporters of the Bloc in Asmara, Massawa, and Decamere; an open assault was made on the village of a district chief . . . who supported the Bloc; Italian farms were raided and ransacked; and the livestock of Moslem tribesmen was looted. The climax came in February when, as the United Nations Commission was arriving, violent fighting broke out in Asmara between Moslems and Christians. It persisted for five days before order was restored and resulted in a long casualty list and wounded.[2]

Lest the purpose of an atrocity be misunderstood, the terrorists often left notes at the scene of the crime threatening death to other bloc supporters.

While the terror succeeded in re-converting virtually all the unionist apostates, it did not, surprisingly, have the coincident effect of firmly cementing the Muslim bloc. Rather, bloc members managed to subordinate their hatred of the unionists to fear, mistrust, and contempt for each other.

In early 1950, shortly after the arrival of the United Nations commission which would propose the colony's future, the bloc smashed itself into three pieces. The precipitating causes were Eritrean suspicion of the Italian connection, heightened by unionist propaganda and Italian exuberance, and a latent struggle for power between Tegray tribal leaders and Ibrahim Sultan who, though a townsman, was believed to harbor ambitions for the leadership of all the Tegrays. On these issues the Muslims split, with the western Tegrays going off on their own to demand, for their chunk of the colony, independence preceded by a period of British trusteeship. In the meantime, a portion of the Christian separatists broke away for a second attempt at accommodation with the unionists. Although the two Christian factions did not negotiate a formal alliance, the rebels, having apparently received modest encouragement from Addis Ababa, set up shop as the Liberal Unionist party with a platform of "conditional" or federal union.

Under the terms of the Italian peace treaty, the Big Four obligated themselves to seek agreement on the disposal of the former Italian colonies and, failing agreement, to refer the issue to the United Nations General Assembly and thereafter to implement its recommendations. Following three years of maneuvering worthy of a Byzantine court, the erstwhile allies achieved uniform agreement on one proposition only: their inability to agree. So, as provided in the treaty, the issue was bumped over to the General Assembly where, surrounded by the lesser states and joined by the two concerned parties—Ethiopia and Italy—they all persisted in denouncing each other's proposals.

Ignoring the prior exertions of the Big Four commission which had visited Eritrea in 1948 and found the population evenly divided between supporters of union and advocates of a transition to independence,* the United Nations sent out its own commission. Its members managed to develop a level of mutual hostility quite rivaling that of their Big Four predecessors and, in consequence of their cordial ill will, to produce two separate reports and three sets of proposals.

One report concluded that only a minority favored independence; the other report found a majority so disposed. The three proposals, reduced to their essence, were (1) union with Ethiopia, (2) federation with Ethiopia, and (3) independence preceded by a ten-year trusteeship under United Nations administration. Unaided even by a statement of the basic facts that commission members agreed on and no doubt weary of the perplexing struggles convulsing this distant and obscure place, the United Nations chose the nominal middle way. It resolved that Eritrea should "constitute an autonomous unit federated with Ethiopia under the sovereignty of the Ethiopian Crown." The Eritrean government was to have full "legislative, executive, and judicial powers in the field of domestic affairs"; an undefined entity designated the "Federal Government," which was to be directed by a federal legislature with proportionate Eritrean representation, was to have jurisdiction over defense, foreign affairs, finance, and foreign and interstate commerce and communications. The resolution provided finally for a two-year transition during which the British administration would assist a United Nations commissioner to fashion the new political structure.[3]

The Short, Unhappy Life of Federation

Eduardo Matienzo of Bolivia, the appointed commissioner, arrived in Eritrea on February 9, 1951, to find that communal hatred and the related resurgence of sheer banditry was cutting a swath of death and devastation across the face of the colony. His appearance had all the impact on the colony's hemorrhage of Canute's proclamation to the sea. It took over a year for the United Nations administration — with Ethiopian government support, terror no longer appearing useful — to reduce both mercenary and political banditry to manageable proportions. Only then was Matienzo able to begin the process of negotiating a constitutional framework.

Even assuming the greatest good will on all sides (an assumption wholly unwarranted by the facts), achievement of a viable federa-

---

*This finding was condemned on several dubious grounds by the French and Russians who, for various reasons, were in 1948 eager to impose an Italian trusteeship.

tion seemed remote. It would exist at the Emperor's sufferance, and he had been opposed from the beginning. Given the nature of his government, a centralized autocracy, as well as the historic tension in Ethiopia between center and periphery, continued opposition was predictable.

No one could accuse the Emperor even of much transitional hypocrisy. Rather than quietly conceding the General Assembly a decent interval to forget that it had, in substance, consigned Eritrea to imperial whim, he reached immediately for control. His representative at the constitutional discussions opposed a federal constitution, insisting that federal authority be lodged in the existing imperial government. Since that government had no legislature, the demand was a little hard to reconcile with the provision in the General Assembly resolution that Eritreans be represented in a federal legislature "in the proportion that the population of Eritrea bears to the population of the Federation."[4] That little difficulty was avoided by the simple expedient of ignoring the reference to a legislature.

Perhaps one should not condemn Matienzo too harshly. He had no mandate to draft a federal constitution, only one for Eritrea. Moreover, he was required to obtain Ethiopian as well as Eritrean approval of his draft.

While deferring to the Emperor's will on the matter of a federal legislature, Matienzo held firm against other Ethiopian demands which would have ripped out the barest essentials of local autonomy. The Emperor was not given the power he sought to appoint all executive officials and to approve or reject all local legislation, a demand which even a majority of the unionists opposed. The Emperor was also frustrated in his efforts to impose on Eritrea the official language of the empire—Amharic—in place of Arabic, preferred by the Muslims, and Tigrinya.

It was in the course of the constitutional negotiations that the first cracks began to appear in the imperial-unionist front. From its inception, the relationship must have been more one of convenience than love. The Emperor was, after all, an Amharic-speaking Shoan. Shoans predominated among his noble and bureaucratic favorites and were the leading recipients of his lavish patronage. He was not, therefore, the most attractive emperor the Christian Tigres could visualize. But Emperor he was and that made him the only available guarantor of Italian and Muslim subordination. The Tigres may have felt like the Polish communist who was asked whether he regarded the Russians as brothers or friends. "Brothers, of course!" he snapped. "One chooses one's friends."

After the guarantee of Christian ascendancy was, in effect, insti-
tutionalized by the United Nations resolution, the analogy became
increasingly apt. Slowly, but not altogether imperceptibly, many
unionists began to slide toward support of a genuine federation.

While the unionists were entertaining belated second thoughts
about the merits of unconditional union, the two Muslim factions
labored successfully to sustain their deep mutual hostility. Their
division, their respective acceptance of the federal concept, and
the shift of opinion in the unionist camp cumulatively produced
opportunities for coalition politics. These opportunities were real-
ized at the end of 1952 after the first — and as it turned out the
last — election under the democratic constitution when the Muslim
Tegrays from western Eritrea joined the unionists to form a majority coalition in the new assembly.

The alliance, bridging seven years of continuous and a millennium of intermittent hostility, created the basis for effective government. To no end. The Emperor, having failed in the constitutional
negotiations to abort autonomy, set about suffocating it. Over the
next ten years, through bribery, intimidation, and where necessary
(as it often was) naked force, the Emperor stripped away the em-
blems and gutted the substance of democracy and autonomy, both
of which he appeared to loathe. On November 14, 1962, following
a rigged parliamentary vote, the chief administrator of Eritrea announced its unconditional union with Ethiopia. The charade was
over. The rebellion had already begun.

It germinated during the late 1950s in Cairo where two veterans
of the antiunionist campaign — Ibrahim Sultan Ali and Woldeab
Woldemariam — had taken refuge. Before federation, Woldemariam had led a small trade union movement, the Christian separatists, and — as evidenced by the failure of six attempts to assassinate
him — a charmed life. Following Britain's withdrawal, the environment for political activities became still less salubrious. The Ethiopian authorities banned formal political parties, and associations
with political overtones were informally hamstrung.

Labor union activities became equally perilous. With an Ethiopian garrison on hand to work his will, the Emperor suppressed
the Eritrean General Union of Labour Syndicates, which Woldemariam had directed. And when, in the post-federation depression, this proved insufficient to quell labor unrest, more direct
measures were available. In February, 1958, a general strike in Asmara and Massawa was crushed by troops who killed and wounded
dozens and arrested hundreds. Thus tranquility was restored.

Apparently unwilling to alter his line of work in ways which
would attract imperial favor, Woldemariam left for Cairo where,

with Ibrahim Sultan Ali, he founded the Eritrean Democratic Front.[5] Initially, its strategy may have been primarily political; Eritreans seem to have had some difficulty in annulling a touching faith in the United Nations' willingness to look after its progeny. At various low points of the cryptofederal experience, Eritreans had futilely petitioned the United Nations for assistance. The requisite third-party concern was unavailable. The United Nations, then as now, was generally insensitive to a member state's domestic pecadillos.

Despite the brutality of Italy's conquest and six-year occupation of Ethiopia, the Emperor left the settler community in peace. So Eritrea ceased to be an object of serious concern in Rome.

There was, of course, an abundance of concern in Washington once work went forth on the huge communications and intelligence-monitoring base complex, Kagnew Station, authorized by the 1953 military and economic assistance agreement between the United States and the imperial Ethiopian government. But Washington's concern was for order, not justice.

So whatever the original intention of its founders, the Eritrean Democratic Front soon went looking for guns. And it took a name appropriate to armed struggle: the Eritrean Liberation Front (ELF). Scrounging together £6500, the ELF purchased a consignment of superannuated Italian rifles and in late 1961 opened the conflict with a scattering of hit-and-run engagements.

Toward National Liberation

In order to trace the thirteen-year course of the insurrection to its present state, one must pass through a jungle of conflicting claims surrounded by marshy data. This is, of course, true in varying degrees for every civil war. The monopoly of violence being the most salient feature of public authority, "legitimate" or "constitutional" governments must minimize the insurgents' achievements or attribute them to the activities of foreign agents. The insurgents, conversely, must seek to enhance their charms and status by emphasizing their indigenous character and by magnifying their political and military operations. In this way, they attract domestic fence-straddlers and foreign support while discouraging external assistance to the incumbents.

Guerrilla tactics magnify a hundredfold these innate obstacles to an accurate account of civil armed conflict. Guerrillas live by mobility and secrecy. Their operational bases are hidden or remote. The nature of their operations — small, scattered units; dif-

ficult communications; a political leadership often compelled to
operate far from the zone of combat — guarantees an operational
diffusion of authority.

The historian's frustrations are further amplified when the rebellion erupts in a Third World state with an autocratic government, for in that case the local press is a mouth organ of of-
ficialdom and the foreign press is rarely there. In the case of
Eritrea, the problem is additionally complicated by the phenom-
enon of endemic banditry and, in certain areas, inter-village loot-
ing which would assure a certain level of violent incidents even if the
ELF did not exist. For all of these reasons, there is to this day very
little hard data about such matters as the size and ideology of ELF
cadres, the number of part-time fighters, and the extent of Chris-
tian-Muslim cooperation.

How much can confidently be said about the insurgency?
There is a consensus about the broad outline of the movement's
evolution. Its launching was facilitated by a recession-bred mi-
gration in the 1950s of workers from Asmara and the port cities
to Saudi Arabia and the Sudan. The workers, plus young Muslims who went to Cairo for a university education, formed a pool
of latent militants who could be organized beyond the Emperor's
reach. A second early asset was the 1962 eruption of civil war in
the Yemen. Weapons from patrons poured into and overflowed
the arsenals of the Yemeni belligerents. Some of these weapons
filtered into the hands of the ELF.

By 1964-65, the movement began to receive a dribble of
direct assistance. Its initial patrons were several Arab League
states — particularly the Sudan and Syria — and perhaps the People's Republic of China. During this period of incipient external
support, the ELF claimed for the first time to have moved beyond
organizational activity and sporadic raids on government outposts
to the actual administration of liberated areas. It also announced
the division of Eritrea into five *wilayat* ("zones"), each under the
control of a military commander. One sign of increased guerilla activity in 1965 was the Ethiopian government's accusation of Syrian
intervention in the empire's internal affairs. Up to that point, the
government had attempted to smother the movement with official
indifference. All violent acts were attributed simply to *shifta* ("bandits").

Consistent with this public posture, the army was prevented
from launching search-and-destroy operations. While officially
ignoring the insurgency, the authorities continued the policy of
currying support primarily among Christian Eritreans with doses
of development funds and imperial patronage.

Despite the government's calm front, it apparently sensed the progressive deterioration of control over the province. One demonstration of its concern was sub rosa discussions with the Sudanese government. In return for reduced support of the ELF, Ethiopia offered to curtail assistance which Israel was funneling through Ethiopia to the southern Sudanese insurrectionists, the Anya'nya. This diplomatic initiative bore fruit in 1967 at roughly the same time that the Ethiopian army was unleashed for the first time. Air and ground forces swept through suspected ELF areas—all of which were populated predominantly by Muslims— burning villages and generating refugees. One authority put the number of burned villages at over 300 and the refugees at over 30,000.

The Emperor had inadvertently chosen a propitious moment to strike. Within five months of the opening of the anti-insurgent campaign, Israel launched the six-day war. By smashing the Arab armies and planting its flag at the Jordan River and the Suez Canal, Israel trivialized Arab interest in events on the periphery of the Middle East.

The only promising development in an otherwise grim year for the ELF was the triumph in Aden of the National Liberation Front. With guerrilla bases in the Sudan largely closed thanks to the Emperor's diplomacy, Aden would become a valuable staging base for the movement of arms and munitions.

Not unnaturally, by the end of 1967 Ethiopian officials believed they had broken the movement's back. In fact, it was at least a year before the ELF was able to demonstrate that news of its demise was premature. The reorganization and rearmament of its forces began slowly in 1968, then seems to have accelerated the following year when Muammar el-Qaddafi and his fellow officers seized power in Libya. The new Libyan regime, militantly pan-Islamic, soon adopted the Eritrean movement. Arms were transported to Southern Yemen, then whisked across the narrow sea to scattered points on the long Eritrean coast. Another 1969 coup, this one in the Sudan, produced a regime less willing to accommodate Ethiopian imperatives. The Sudanese pipeline and sanctuary were temporarily reopened.

While beginning again to flex their muscles in the bush, the insurgents opened a new front with a series of attacks on Ethiopian Airlines planes. The campaign began in March of 1969 and persisted into 1972, when it culminated in a bloody shootout several thousand feet over Addis. All seven ELF agents, five men and two women (including several university students), were shot to death by government agents within seconds after the hijacking was announced. The ferocity of the scene was described by an

American professor who was aboard the plane and was himself wounded by a grenade fragment. "The last thing I saw before the firing stopped," he said, "was a beautiful Ethiopian girl crawling by the row of seats in which I was crouched. She had a grenade in the hand she was using to push herself along and she was using her other hand in a futile effort to staunch the blood flowing out of her side. She died a few feet up the aisle."

This aborted hijacking was a microcosm of events in Eritrea at the second peak of the insurgent challenge. Throughout 1969, insurgent activities multiplied. Roads were mined; small police and army units were ambushed; the U.S. consul-general in Asmara was kidnapped, subjected to a lecture on the movement, then released. The imperial government responded in the spring of 1970 by again unleashing the Second Division for a bout of destruction. This time, however, the carnage earned only a brief respite. By late summer, the government's version of security was on a downward spiral. One district governor was killed in a brush with guerrillas. Bridges were blown up. The roads were alive with ambushes; the division commander stumbled into one of them and was killed. The armed forces responded with a rampage through nearby villages, massacring hundreds. A civilian governor who had generally opposed high-profile military operations was replaced by a general. The imperial authorities slapped martial law on most of the province, and the army and air force expanded the zone of their destructive operations. A largely Muslim town was pulverized from the air. Sweeps continued. There were no official reports of battles lost and won, but that some were fought was evidenced by a flow of military casualties into the army hospitals of Asmara.

The immediate and longer term impact of the Ethiopian army's 1970-71 campaign is uncertain. For the short term, it apparently effected a sharp reduction in insurgent military operations. But in the process it may, in the traditional way of anti-insurgent forces, have enhanced popular receptivity to the ELF's program. One local Ethiopian official complained to Bowyer Bell, a student of the insurgency: "All we're doing is alienating the countryside, making the population more bitter than it was before."[6] Elsewhere Bell describes the imperial army as "contemptuous of the people in the Eritrean province and apparently [regarding] the Muslims especially with suspicion and distaste."[7]

While it therefore appears that the 1970-71 campaign prepared the ground for yet more determined and comprehensive uprisings, events conspired to slow its growth. First, the Emperor, quick as ever to exploit opportunity, reduced the ELF's access to foreign support. Paradoxically, it was Gen. Gaafar Mohammed Nimeri's decision to conciliate his southern insurrectionaries by granting them a considerable degree of autonomy which enabled Haile Selassie to narrow if not altogether close the Sudanese door for his northern insurgents. When the Emperor extended his good offices to the Sudanese belligerents to facilitate their peace negotiations, Nimeri responded by withdrawing semiofficial support from the liberation movement. The length of the border and pockets of loyal sympathy for the movement kept the frontier permeable, but the Sudan's value as a base area had been reduced.

A second blow was the establishment of full diplomatic ties with the Chinese, who coincidentally declared that it was not their policy to support subversion of governments with whom they enjoyed formal relations. Whatever the generic validity of that declaration, I was assured by one of the best-informed diplomats in Addis that the Chinese have terminated all assistance to the ELF, an assurance consistent with the uniformly favorable attention bestowed on the Chinese by the government-controlled press in Addis.

A third initiative was directed toward the government of the People's Democratic Republic of Yemen (PDRY). It was reminded that the large Yemeni population in Ethiopia and its valuable remittances to relatives in the PDRY existed at the Emperor's sufferance. While this warning did not eliminate Aden as a transshipment point for Libyan and other arms, it allegedly produced a lower level of open cooperation in the arms traffic.

While trying through the instrument of diplomacy to isolate the ELF cadres from the outside world, the Emperor moved simultaneously to cut their domestic ties by measures of tactical conciliation. No concessions were made on the basic issue of autonomy or representative government; but the army was again reined in, and some additional funds were provided for reconstruction and development, largely, it appears, in areas where Christians predominated.

While the Emperor was trying to kill it, the ELF on its own initiative took a fling at self-destruction. Divisive tensions wrack every liberation movement. They spring from many sources: abrasions between fighting units and the political directorate ensconced in some friendly foreign capital far from the zone of danger and unsure of its control; the temptations offered by competing, often mutually antagonistic, foreign patrons; disputes over the terms of settlement and the anticipated allocation of victory's benefits; difficulties of communication and supply; and the inevitable defectors and informants who intensify the para-

noia native to an underground struggle. The ELF demonstrated
all of these generic tensions plus others which vary with time and
place. One of the variables which has haunted the Eritrean insurgency is the lack of a pre-existing sense of common identity or
purpose in the population base from which the insurgents spring,
a characteristic common to most African rebellions. There is,
more precisely, neither a profound sense of nationalism nor a
shared ideological experience to help activists in overcoming
clan, class, linguistic, regional, religious, and personal differences. Nor is there a single charismatic leader.

External forces have aggravated indigenous sources of discord. For instance, initial support from Saudi Arabia allegedly
was withdrawn because Christian participation diluted the element of pan-Islamic nationalism in the movement. A comparable
desire to pull the ELF into a belligerently Islamic orientation, as
well as distaste for its acceptance of aid and training from
nominal or actual Marxist countries, may explain fluctuations in
the measure of Libyan support.

Discord between patrons has not been located exclusively
along the fault lines of religion and ideology. Syria and Iraq are
both Muslim and rhetorically socialist. That coincidence has mel-
lowed neither their mutual contempt nor their competitive patronage of the liberation movement.

In the face of its internal tensions and their external irritants,
sustained unity within the ELF would have been miraculous.
There having been no divine intervention, in 1968-69 the movement splintered. Outside Eritrea, there appeared two organized
fragments, the ELF-General Command and the ELF-Popular
Forces which may or may not have included all of the fighting
bands. The competitors quickly associated themselves, respectively, with Baghdad and Damascus. Notwithstanding claims to the
contrary, in fact very little is known about the real differences
between the two movements.

At the time of the split, Osman Saleh Sabbe, the leading
figure in the Popular Forces, and his General Command rivals
indicted each other for associating with reactionary regimes and
for being representative of backward, tribal, and exclusively
Muslim elements in Eritrea. The Popular Forces specifically accused the General Command of assassinating two Christian
members of the ELF while the General Command anathematized
Saleh Sabbe and his associates for remaining outside Eritrea during the bitter fighting ignited in 1967-68 by Ethiopia's first big
push against the insurgents. Saleh Sabbe, apparently conceding
that the split was, at least in part, one between local military

commanders and the political leadership, accused the General Command activists of having failed to follow orders during that period.

Reports of bloody shootouts between Muslim and Christian bands as well as of confessional antagonism (for example, a refusal to eat together) within nominally integrated guerrilla units under-lined the reality of Muslim-Christian hostility. The externally based political arms of the insurgency, however, appeared rather to bridge than to mirror this sharp division. Both now have a sub-stan-tial number of Christian members. U.S. government sources ex-press the belief that there are proportionately more Christians in the Popular Liberation Forces (PLF) which are more leftist ideo-logically, a characteristic which tends toward the transcendence of religious animosity.

Despite their internal struggles, within two years the insurgents, although badly wounded by the Ethiopian army's offensive in 1970-71, had mounted a new and yet more serious threat to imperial au-thority. Incidents of violence multiplied, spurring a perceptible mi-gration of Italian capital and driving a Japanese firm to suspend copper-mining activities. By the summer of 1974, the distinguished British journalist, Colin Legum, returned from the Horn and an-nounced: "There can no longer be any serious hope of defeating the rebels by military force. The only practical question now is what kind of political settlement is possible."[8] Virtually no one in the country with any claim to objectivity disagreed.

Notes

For information on the history and ethnology of Eritrea, the author is particu-larly indebted to G. K. N. Trevaskis, *Eritrea: A Colony in Transition* (London: Oxford University Press, 1960).

1.   Trevaskis, p. 75.

2.   *Ibid,* p. 96.

3.   United Nations, General Assembly, Resolution 390 A (V): Final Report of the United Nations Commission in Eritrea (Seventh Session, Supplement Number Fifteen A/2188), pp. 74-5.

4.   *Ibid.*

5.   For useful accounts of the insurgency, see *inter alia:* Mordechai Abir, "The Contentious Horn of Africa," *Conflict Studies* 24 (June 1972); J. B. Bell, "Endemic Insurgency and International Order: The Eritrean Experience," *Orbis* 18 (1974):431; J. F. Campbell, "Background to the Eritrean Con-flict." *Africa Report,* May 1971, p. 19; C. Clapham, "Ethiopia and Somalia" in *Conflicts in Africa: Adelphi Papers Number Ninety-three* (London: The International Institute for Strategic Studies, 1972); F. Halliday, "The Fight-ing in Eritrea," *New Left Review,* May-June 1971, p. 57; P. Robbs, "Battle

for the Red Sea," *Africa Report,* March-April 1975, p. 14; and B. Whitaker, ed., *The Fourth World* (New York: Schocken Books, 1972) .

6.   *Time,* March 10, 1971, p. 35.

7.   Bell, "Endemic Insurgency," p. 440.

8.   "Ethiopia Losing Hope of Winning Eritrean War," *Observer Foreign News Service,* July 9, 1974, p. 1.

After the Revolution: National Socialism 3

Nationalism: Conciliation Confounded

For a number of reasons, there was a widespread expectation that the new government in Ethiopia under the Dergue would seek a political settlement through major concessions. In the first place, the sheer fact that it represented a radical constitutional break with the old order induced the conviction that wherever that order had failed, the Dergue would try out different policies. Second, since the new government seemed committed to a secularized state free of Shoan domination, to the elimination of corruption in provincial as well as national government, and to radical reform generally, it had bases for appealing to the Eritreans that had been utterly unavailable to the Emperor. Secularization would appeal to the Muslim half of the Eritrean population. Radicalization would appeal to that wing of the secessionist movement, allegedly concentrated in the PLF, which had hitherto equated secession with reform. Diffusion of power beyond the Shoan elite could assuage the large Tigrean element in the Eritrean population. Finally, since the decentralization of governmental functions to representative regional institutions had been an anathema to the Emperor, there was a hope that such decentralization would be included in the program of the new order — if for no better reason than the dialectic of reaction and revolution.

Concrete signs gave weight to these speculations. In the late spring of 1974, the Endalkachew government, necessarily acting with the consent if not at the instance of the Dergue, appointed a Christian and a Muslim Eritrean to serve as deputy governors-general in the province. These appointments were followed at the end of August by the selection of a distinguished jurist, Immanuel Andermichael, a nonpolitical Eritrean Christian, as governor-general. The stage seemed set for a major initiative.

Gen. Aman Michael Andom, being, on the one hand, an Eritrean Christian (but from the small Protestant minority within
the Christian community) and, on the other, the hard-nosed
commander of the Ethiopian division that had bashed the
Somalis in 1964, had ideal credentials for reconciling Eritrean
and Ethiopian nationalism. In Eritrea and apparently among
liberation movement leaders in Arab capitals, there was a mood
of high expectation. Everyone seemed to recognize that this was
one of those rare, fleeting moments when it is possible to overcome historical inertia and to break decisively with the past.

Within Eritrea, there was a palpable lull in hostilities. The
scent of a settlement, coupled with the Second Division's passivity, drew the guerrillas out of their myriad rural hideouts
toward the main towns and cities. With peace seemingly in the
offing or, alternatively, with an opportunity for more effective
war should the revolution produce the collapse of authority at
the center, a rash of talks broke out among the hostile wings of
the liberation movement.

General Aman moved quickly to seize the day. Through the
good offices of President Nimeri, whose naturally pro-Muslim
sentiments were inevitably qualified by ambivalence about secessionist movements, Aman opened negotiations with spokesmen
for the insurgents. Although the precise terms of his overture
have never been officially announced, it appears that he proposed internal autonomy for all of Eritrea except the port of
Assab and possibly a strip of land connecting Assab to the highlands. The port and access route would remain under the direct
authority of Addis. Both movements responded with a public reaffirmation of their commitment to full independence. Yet Western sources continued to believe that important elements in the
movement, particularly many Christians, would settle for less.

Perhaps they were right. We will never know, because some time
on November 23, 1974 — "Bloody Saturday" as it is now remembered — an army unit arrived at General Aman's villa and announced that by order of the Dergue he was under arrest. When
Aman refused to submit, an intense firefight erupted. The inhabitants of the villa fought desperately and, for a while, successfully.
Then tanks, called in by the conspirators, crashed through the thick
walls that had protected the defenders.

The subsequent official account declared that the general had
died resisting arrest. But some in Addis believed that, in the grand
Ethiopian tradition, he had chosen suicide over capture. By
whatever means, he perished. And with him perished two young

members of the Dergue, close to sixty of the imprisoned paladins of the old regime, and the hope for peace in Eritrea.

The particular event which allegedly galvanized the general's opponents to stage this coup within the revolutionary coup was his refusal to dispatch additional troops to Eritrea, a gambit guaranteed to snap the sprig of conciliation. Apparently, there was a great deal of discord in the government and Aman's refusal represented only a small part of it. Rightly or wrongly—events suggest rightly—General Aman was identified with the "moderate" position on every important conflicted issue. He was thought to oppose summary justice for the elite and to support a flexible and discriminating land reform and a pluralistic government as well as a negotiated settlement in Eritrea. Differences over these fundamental issues, sufficient in themselves to trigger fratricide, were aggravated by the deep insecurity of all the main actors. Together they had overthrown in a historical instant the accumulated institutions of a millennium. In so doing, they had created virtually a political state of nature. The traditional sources of authority were in ruins. No one knew where power lay, who would obey what order. Conceivably, with one daring thrust, any of the factions within the armed forces could eliminate the others. As in the condition of unstable deterrence between nuclear powers, everyone feared a first strike.

Deliberations of the Dergue and the individual views of its members remain a riddle buried in an enigma. It is still impossible to tell whether Maj. Mengistu Haile Mariam and Lt. Col. Atnafu Abate, the apparent leaders of the anti-Aman thrust, opposed any concessions which would create a special status for Eritrea or became discouraged at the initial Eritrean response and concerned about the perceptible accretions of strength to the liberation movement during the de facto stand-down. Perhaps both precipitants were at work. Or perhaps Aman's opponents concluded simply that the liberation movements had to be badly bloodied before they would negotiate on acceptable terms. Bloodying the insurgents had systematically failed in the past. But in the past the alternative to struggle had been capitulation to an intolerable imperial order. As a prelude to compromise negotiated in the context of a revolutionized society, the conspirators may have concluded it could work.

And so within hours of Aman's death, trucks crowded with reinforcements for the 10,000 men of the Second Division rumbled through the streets of Addis. The reinforcements may also have been intended to neutralize that division if, following news of Aman's death, it decided to impose order not on Eritrea but on Addis.

The Eritreans responded with a coordinated assault in the very heart of Asmara. It was war *à outrance.*

Christians and Muslims, Marxists and conservatives, ELF and PLF, these distinctions no longer mattered. For the first time one could speak without baroque hyperbole of a "people's war." And since it was the "people" who were making war on them, the Ethiopian armed forces began unequivocally making war on the "people." Outside the major cities, the Ethiopian air force in its American planes, flown by American-trained pilots, dropped American bombs on the towns and villages where the insurgents were or might have been or might soon be. Within Asmara, suspected insurgents began to die violently. The only rule of war recognized by either side was efficacy.

With the struggle entering a seemingly apocalyptic phase, the Arab states finally began to show signs of broader and unembarrassed support. A government spokesman in the parliament of impeccably conservative Kuwait assured his listeners that the government would not stand by while fellow Muslims were massacred and hinted broadly of extensive aid. The Saudis also claimed that they were assisting the insurgents. When a delegation sent by the Dergue to major Arab capitals failed to secure assurances of nonintervention, Addis began to complain openly and with increasing bitterness of Arab intervention.

Each side seemed to exaggerate. Although apparently well-equipped with mines, small arms, and machine guns, the liberation forces still failed to display very much in the way of an effective riposte to armor and air power. The really sophisticated instruments of modern insurgency, hand-carried anti-tank and anti-aircraft weapons, were not deployed in substantial quantities. On the Arab side, support was still a good deal more rhetorical than real. At least there remained plenty of room for escalation.

After the assault on Asmara itself had been blunted, liberation movement forces continued to operate nearby and to threaten the thin supply routes to the highlands and the coast. For a short time, it even seemed possible that the insurgents might succeed in strangling the Ethiopian forces based in the city. But in the end, their inability to hold off armor and to reduce their vulnerability to air power assured continued Ethiopian control of the major cities and most of the towns. Those that could not be controlled could at least be devastated by bombardment and temporary occupation whenever the insurgents attempted to make a stand. Without a major qualitative step-up in external assistance, the insurgents seemed unable to enter the phase of sustained frontal combat with large units of the imperial armed forces.

By the spring of 1975, the antagonists were plainly stalemated. Addis could neither occupy the countryside nor decimate the insurgents. The insurgents could not take any of the principal cities nor hold the towns nor indefinitely block the supply routes.

After the terrible slaughter of the prior few months, the avenue of conciliation seemed hopelessly blocked. For the insurgents, the only ways out seemed to be a massive escalation of external support, another outbreak of fratricide in the Dergue, a mutiny against the Dergue by one or more of the divisions in the field, or a U.S. decision to close its military pipeline to the Dergue. One further possibility was the gradual fabrication of operational links with anti-Dergue forces in other provinces, a development now reportedly under way. For the Dergue, on the other hand, the only perceived through-route was the familiar one murderously pioneered by predecessors in the counterinsurgency game: drain the rural sea, and the guerrilla fish will die.

Hitherto, divisions of opinion, particularly in the Christian community, on the virtues of independence had been a source of constraint on Ethiopian strategy. More highly educated than any other element in the Ethiopian mosaic, enjoying the commercial sophistication common among peoples of trading coasts, drawn painfully into the modern world through the medium of the colonial experience, Eritreans were disproportionately represented in public administration and commerce throughout the empire. Even in the armed forces, particularly the navy, they were not unrepresented, though their number had dwindled as the civil war intensified. Addis alone was thought to have an Eritrean population in excess of 100,000.

Before Aman's death, a large proportion of the Eritrean Christian elite seemed antagonistic to the demand for complete independence, although many apparently preferred some degree of home rule. But after the fall of Aman and the insurgent offensive, these moderates began tumbling toward the secessionist pole. In Eritrea, whole detachments of the locally recruited and officered police deserted to the countryside after assisting in the release of movement prisoners. Elsewhere in the empire, Eritreans, particularly students, began drifting back to their homes where their only possible occupation would be insurgency.

Having at last converted the great mass of Eritreans into the enemy, the masters of Addis could now pursue the logic of counterinsurgency to its murderous end. The loss of constraint coin-

cided felicitously with the arrival of opportunity. The drought
which had devastated Wallo and Tigre now tightened its grip on
Eritrea. To be sure, the government by this time had a functioning relief agency. And there was food for it to distribute. But this
little impediment to conscripting famine as an ally was overcome
by fiat: the agency would not function in rural Eritrea. The
Dergue also ordered foreign and international relief agencies to
close their feeding stations in the countryside. Food in excess of
the needs of the garrisons and, barely, the population of the occupied urban areas has now been barred from the province.

Thus far, nature seems to have thwarted the vicious purposes
of men. According to reports, the most recent harvest has been
relatively bountiful. The fact remains that the government of
Ethiopia, with careful premeditation, tried to orchestrate the
starvation of Eritrea's rural population. This did not deter that
celebrated moralist, the U.S. secretary of state, from vetoing proposals that eliminated Ethiopia from the military assistance program. In fact, U.S. military assistance to Ethiopia is projected at
$41.9 million, an increase of $4.3 million over 1975. Meanwhile,
most congressmen who normally are sensitive to the human rights
dimensions of allegedly strategic issues seem indifferent to the
plight of the Eritreans. The political and human rights organs of
the United Nations are equally mute.

Authoritarian Socialism: Reform by Bayonet

The torrents of revolution poured through the gap created by
Aman's death and engulfed almost sixty leaders of the old order.
With a few exceptions—notably the last two prime ministers,
Aklilu Habte-Wold and Endalkachew Makonnen—they seemed
to have been drawn almost at random from the collection of dignitaries marooned in the Fourth Division's barracks. In groups of
ten, they were hustled through the quiet campsite to hear a sen-
tence of death pronounced by the staccato chatter of machine
guns.

Although the primary reason for this freshet of executions probably was to distract attention from the blow against Aman, it also
effectively signaled a decisive turn in the revolution. The hasty men
of iron had won. Social transformation would be conducted from
the top and, like the war in Eritrea, through the medium of bayo-
nets. There would be no compromise, no equivocation.

If, following the massacre, any doubt remained on this score,
it was soon dissipated by the land reform decree. Announcement

of the reform had been awaited with breathless expectancy. In Ethiopia, land is pretty close to everything: it is the margin of existence for the peasant masses who comprise over eighty percent of the population; it is the state's primary source of foreign exchange; it is the symbol of social hierarchy and the reward for loyal servants of the regime.[1] For decades, the land question had haunted Ethiopian political life. Foreign advisers of every political and ideological stripe had proclaimed it the key to the country's putative potential as the breadbasket of the Middle East.* It was enthroned in imperial and parliamentary rhetoric. There was even a Ministry of Land Reform. But, like a child's toy car resting on its back while its wheels spin, there was no perceptible forward movement.

There was no mystery in the Emperor's studied failure to approach closer than hailing distance to reform. Significant change in land tenure meant trouble, personal loss, or both. Who, after all, were the leading landowners? The imperial family, the church, the nobility, a host of provincial gentry, and senior figures on both the civilian and military sides of the regime—in short, most of the politically sentient elements of the realm. There is no evidence that any of them yearned for a reduction either in the rents they were entitled to extract or in the size of their holdings. The imperial holdings not only yielded rents to supplement funds that, though nominally public, were equally at the Emperor's disposal but, in addition, provided a reservoir of land available to reward useful functionaries, to satiate the ambitious, and to corrupt incipient reformers.

In the decade preceding the Emperor's fall, agricultural modernization, encouraged by the World Bank and the U.S. Agency for International Development (USAID), had, if anything, stiffened resistance to egalitarian reform. Modernization meant consolidation of holdings (often by the removal of tenants), mechanization, and production for export. The result was vastly increased land values and a major increment in foreign exchange earnings. Coffee and leguminous crops were favored. The high prices generally prevailing in the early seventies, particularly for pulses, together with the sharp increase in production were largely responsible for the comfortable foreign exchange surplus that was the Emperor's unintended bequest to his militant young heirs.

---

*This euphoric prophesy has been lowered, as the highland's topsoil has washed away, to a capacity to feed Ethiopia's 26 million people and to provide modest, though still essential experts.

Reform was not only threatening to the whole, seemingly stable structure of power; in addition, it was hellishly complicated. Land-holding patterns were at least as diverse as the ethnic mosaic. In many cases, they were also obscure both physically and juridically. There were no formal surveys, no land registration, few records of any kind. No William the Conqueror had ever appeared to sort things out. And if one had tried, he might soon have expired from frustration.

At best, one could say that there were general tendencies in different regions. In the northern plateau, including Tigre and the Christian highlands of Eritrea, much land was held communally, though farmed individually; and plots were exchanged at regular intervals to promote an even distribution of the land's bounty. In several of the southern, predominantly Galla provinces, the pattern was at the other end of the continuum of equity. These were the territories taken by conquest rather than elite assimilation. Most of the conquering had been accomplished within the past century by Menelik II. The tenants, groaning under rents trampolining as high as two-thirds of each crop, were the descendants of the former owners, the subjugated Gallas. The owners, sometimes absentee, were in many cases the descendants of the very soldiers who had done the subjugating. Between landlord and tenant, divided by class interest, culture, and history, tension always ran high. Here was the classic terrain for equitable reform. Between these two extremes, tenure displayed stunning variations. There were, in effect, individual landowners who might or might not pay some fee in kind to another person or an institution with residual claims. In the case of a clear tenancy, such matters as the size of the rent, the landlord's services (seed, animals, credit, etc.), and stability of tenure varied extensively.

These intimidating complexities seemed almost to defy generally applicable legislation. Not surprisingly, the men who had dealt so summarily with General Aman's defiance showed no less capacity for decision in this instance. They simply proclaimed the nationalization of all rural land. Henceforth, it was to be "the collective property of the Ethiopian People." Title being simplified through this bold rhetorical stroke, ergo general legislation became possible.

All the pre-existing rights of landlords were abolished. Compensation would be paid only for machinery. The large commercial farms would be managed by the state; other holdings would be farmed communally. And to that end, peasants were urged to form associations immediately.

Soon thereafter, the government announced that the entire student population of the university in Addis and of the senior secondary schools would be dispatched to the countryside to assist in implementing the decreed reforms and to promote modernization. Not all students embraced this sudden, heroic opportunity with unqualified zeal. Student opposition flowed in part from the absence of prior consultation and the anticipation of rude conditions of life in the Stone Age countryside. There was, as well, the dark suspicion that the Dergue's overriding motive was to remove a rumbling source of opposition from the center of power.

Throughout the sixties and on into the seventies, as the student population had multiplied, relations between students and the various elements of the security forces were decidedly on the ragged side. As a group, the former were the one consistent center of root-and-branch opposition to the established order of things, although by virtue of receiving a higher education they were assured a comparatively comfortable place in it. Over the years they had at intervals been clubbed, gassed, imprisoned, expelled, and, on occasion, shot down by security forces sent to pacify demonstrations or terminate subversive meetings.

When the armed forces had at last moved against the Emperor, the students had rallied in support. But although it is probable that at least a few of the younger officers had attended the university and virtually all shared the students' desire for the modernization of Ethiopia, during the turbulent months preceding the Emperor's fall, the Dergue, swathed in secrecy, remained aloof.

The sense of being as much outside the ambit of decision-making as passive time-servers in the civil service must have galled the young men and women who, after years of student protests, undoubtedly saw themselves as the true vanguard of the revolution. Gall was succeeded by deep concern once the character of the new order became manifest following Aman's death. An open system in which students, workers, and soldiers would together remake Ethiopia through collective decisions held no apparent allure for the masters of the Dergue.

So some students resisted. Perhaps they would have been joined by many others if the Dergue had not once again demonstrated both its effective control of the means of coercion and its willingness to employ them. Almost a thousand students soon found themselves under detention. The remainder were trucked out into the immense countryside for a rendezvous with the rural masses many miles and in some respects a psychological millennium away.

With the students gone, the only overt challenge to the Dergue's authority came from organized labor. The causes of its unrest had not abated. Prices remained high, wages low. Revolutionary euphoria could fill the stomach for just so long. The new government did not court popularity. It encouraged no pretense. The function of workers was to work. Strikes were forbidden. When the economy improved, they would be rewarded. In the meantime — but this was implicit — the first claims on the bulging national reserves were drought relief, rural reform, and military refurbishment, not necessarily in that order of precedence. When the workers threatened to manifest their disillusion by meetings, pamphleteering, and parades, they discovered that the new rulers were, if anything, less charitable toward dissidence than the Emperor had been.

In September, a year after the Emperor's fall, the Dergue, faced with a general strike-threat from the 125,000-member Ethiopian Labour Confederation, sent its security forces raging through the streets of Addis. Their orders: to arrest anyone distributing the confederation's manifesto condemning the Dergue and demanding the establishment of democratic liberties. When unarmed Ethiopian Airlines employees attempted to prevent the arrest of a coworker engaged in distribution, the security forces opened fire, killing four and wounding twenty-nine. A kind of peace settled again over the capital.

Opposition to the Dergue was not limited to students and workers. Nor was it uniformly unarmed. Particularly in the ruggedly conservative northern provinces of Gojjam and Begemdir — where the Orthodox church was strong, the gentry unruly, and where aristocrat and peasant shared a common culture and an ancient history of, among other things, antagonism to central authority — revolt flowered. Information about its dimensions has been extremely sparse, but reports, even in the government-controlled media, suggest substantial difficulties with "bandits" and enemies of the revolution. Such acts as the murder of a provincial governor and his aide led to the dispatch of soldiers, including members of the elite paratroop unit. The harsh terrain virtually precludes eradication of all local opposition. But at the same time, it must enormously complicate any effort by rebel groups to concert their activities. As long as the Dergue maintains sufficient forces in the area to prevent the formation of a critical mass of opposition, this rural dissidence does not by itself represent a major threat to the regime.

The revolt of the Afar nomads in the eastern lowlands is a considerably more serious matter. Numbering less than 200,000, this very traditional and distinctive people, adherents of Islam, inhabit the forbidding terrain between southern Eritrea and the port of Djibouti.

With the possible exception of the small number of Afars who have entered the modern economy, Afar tribesmen on both sides of the border owe allegiance to Sultan Ali Mireh Hanfare who, like his predecessors, headquartered until June, 1975, in the small oasis town of Asieta located 340 miles east of Addis near the border of the French territory. He had initially given his backing to the Dergue on the understanding that it would generally follow the Emperor's policy of treating the sultan's domain as a de facto semiautonomous fiefdom. It appears that relations began to curdle when, in the course of its desperate offensive in the fall of 1974, the ELF extended its operations into Afar country in the extreme south of Eritrea near the port of Assab. Since it is widely assumed in Ethiopia that, as one diplomat put it, "nothing goes on in Afar territory for very long without the sultan's knowledge or expressed consent,"[2] the Dergue undoubtedly concluded that the sultan was an undependable associate. Perhaps that is one reason it began, as part of the land reform program, to move highlanders down into the Afar grazing lands.

It was a risk and arguably not a very well-calculated one. Nothing short of a direct attack on the sultan was more likely to incite rebellion. And rebellion by the reportedly 5,000 well-armed men subject to the sultan's direction would threaten Ethiopia's two southern lifelines to the Red Sea—the road linking Addis Ababa to Assab and the Franco-Ethiopian railway with its coastal terminus in Djibouti. Periodic interdiction of the route to Massawa, along with its perpetual hazards, had aggravated Addis's dependence on these other two ports. In addition, practically all of the country's petroleum supplies are carried inland by tank trucks from the aging refinery at Assab.

Perhaps it was the vulnerability of the Assab and Djibouti routes, together with the perceived unreliability of the sultan, which led first to the introduction of alien highlanders and then to a build-up of troops. And these considerations may have been compounded by the regime's manifest intolerance of alternative sources of power or authority as well as of every vestige of traditional society. Whatever its motives, the regime's actions had one probable outcome.

It is unclear just what ignited the kindling. One spark would have sufficed. What we do know is that in June, 1975, the Dergue attacked Asieta, reportedly with jet aircraft and tanks, driving the sultan and many of his followers across the border into French territory. At about the same time, Afar warriors damaged a key bridge on the Assab road, producing a run on gasoline supplies in the capital. The interruption of traffic was, however, temporary.

Since then, both the railway line and the road have remained open, a feat which could not have been managed without a large concentration of Ethiopian forces supported by aircraft.

With the Afars in revolt, the Dergue is now faced with enemies along its entire eastern flank: in the north, there are the Eritreans; below them, the Afars; and finally, for over a thousand miles from Djibouti to the Kenya border, the great hereditary foe — the Somalis.

Notes

1.   J. M. Cohen, "Ethiopia After Selassie: The Government Land Factor," *African Affairs* 72 (1973) : 365-82 and R. K. Pankhurst, *State and Land in Ethiopia* (Addis Ababa, 1966) .

2.   *Financial Times,* June 20, 1975, p. 7.

Part Two

Ethiopia and the Somalis

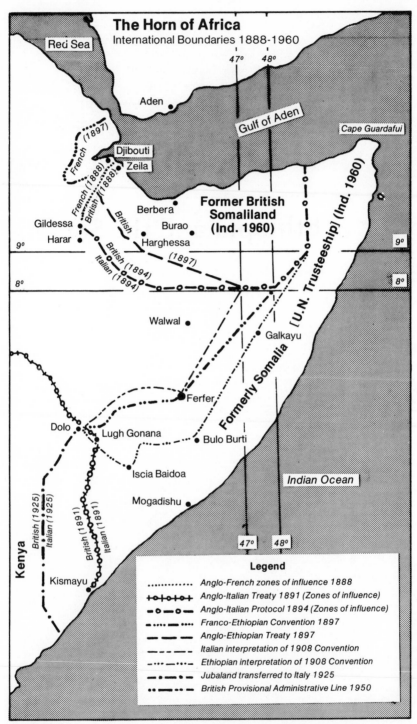

The Horn of Africa
International Boundaries 1888-1960

Red Sea

47° 48°

Aden

Gulf of Aden

Cape Guardafui

(1897)

French (1897)

Djibouti

French (1888)

Zeila

British (1888)

Berbera

Former British
Somaliland
(Ind. 1960)

Gildessa

British

Burao

Harar

Harghessa

9°

British (1894)

British (1897)

Italian (1894)

[U.N. Trusteeship] (Ind. 1960)

9°

8°

8°

Walwal

Galkayu

Ferfer

Formerly Somalia

Dolo

Lugh Gonana

Bulo Burti

Iscia Baidoa

Indian Ocean

Mogadishu

47° 48°

Kenya

British (1925)

Italian (1925)

British (1891)

Italian (1891)

Kismayu

Legend
.... Anglo-French zones of influence 1888
+o+o+o+ Anglo-Italian Treaty 1891 (Zones of influence)
–o–o–o– Anglo-Italian Protocol 1894 (Zones of influence)
–..––..–– Franco-Ethiopian Convention 1897
– – – Anglo-Ethiopian Treaty 1897
–·–·–·– Italian interpretation of 1908 Convention
–··–··– Ethiopian interpretation of 1908 Convention
–··–··– Jubaland transferred to Italy 1925
•• ■ ■ British Provisional Administrative Line 1950

© John Drysdale. *The Somali Dispute* (New York: Praeger, 1964). Reprinted by permission of the publisher.

The Roots of Conflict 4

The Land and People

Peripheral threats to the Ethiopian empire assume a common geometric form. Like the Eritreans, the Somalis occupy a triangular slice of East Africa. Its base is the African littoral of the Gulf of Aden stretching from Djibouti to the easternmost tip of the continent at Cape Guardafui roughly parallel to the southeastern coast of the Arabian Peninsula. Its peak thrusts deeply into northeast Kenya. The Indian Ocean bounds it on one long side, the great East African Rift on the other. The result is an area of some 370,000 square miles, nearly as large as Ethiopia.*

Except in the narrow belt between the two southern rivers, the Juba and the Shebelle, and in the far northwest of the plateau overlapping the political frontier with Ethiopia, the land is an arid savannah, an endless vista of coarse grass punctuated by thorn trees, giant anthills, and the thick-trunked baobabs.

This severe land supports a population variously estimated at three and a half to five million people, about three-quarters of whom are nomadic pastoralists. Though most nomads have sheep, goats, and cattle as well, the camel is king. John Drysdale, a former member of the British colonial administration, explains why:

> The Somali camel, a one-humped beast, can go longer without water than any other breed of camel. In the very driest weather it need not be watered more than once every three weeks. It can

---

* This is the area occupied by the Somali people; the Democratic Republic of Somalia occupies an area of 246,000 square miles.

thus browse a hundred miles or so from the nearest wells.
Herdsmen will drive their camels in the dry season to pastures
seven days distant from the wells, graze them for a week and
march them back again for water; and repeat this perfor-
mance for three or four months between [rainy] seasons. . . .
The nomad subsists during this period entirely on camel's milk.
Not even the morning dew passes between his lips; that he col-
lects to wash himself.[1]

The Somalis are as culturally uniform as the Ethiopians are
mixed. From Djibouti in the north to Kenya's Tana River in the
south, they speak a common language, enjoy a rich oral literature
centered on poetic forms, organize communal life around similar,
egalitarian social institutions, distinguish themselves from their
Bantu and Nilotic neighbors by emphasizing a geneology stretching
back to an original Arab ancestor, and manifest a powerful devotion to Islam. These cultural factors as well as the millennial
occupation of contiguous territory and at least 500 years of intermittent conflict with the Christian occupants of the Ethiopian plateau make for an indisputable shared sense of nationhood. That
sense has survived long association with Hamitic kinsmen who border them on three sides: the Afars (or Danakils) in the north and
the various branches of the Gallas in the west and south. Surviving
as well the political divisions imposed initially during the colonial
scramble and partially sustained—in some ways aggravated—
through the era of decolonization, that sense now constitutes the
root of the Somali problem.

Ethnologists agree that the Somalis made an unambiguous
appearance on the historical stage about A.D. 1000 along the
coast of the Gulf of Aden. During the next 900 years, they
gradually elbowed their way south until, at the turn of the twentieth century, they reached the Tana River.

The word *they* is deceptive if taken to mean a well-organized
collective thrust. Despite their cultural bonds, the Somalis did not
move, think, or act as a political unit. They were divided into a few
great clan-families, subdivided into clans, and then divided once
again into patrilineal kinship groups. Each individual Somali had
some sense of attachment to each of these progressively smaller
hereditary groupings; but as Ian Lewis, a leading British authority
on the Somalis, has noted,

. . . his most binding and most frequently mobilized loyalty is
to his *diya*-paying group. This unit with a fighting strength of
from a few hundred to a few thousand men, consists of close

kinsmen united by a specific contractual alliance whose terms stipulate that they should pay and receive blood-compensation (Arabic, *diya*) in concert. An injury done by or to any member of the group implicates all those who are a party to its treaty. Thus if a man of one group is killed by a man of another, the first group will collectively claim the damages due from the second. At the same time within any group a high degree of co-operation and mutual collaboration prevails.[2]

Originating in the harshest area of the Horn except for the Danakil Depression, the Somalis moved south—and to a limited degree west—in search of pasture and water. There is no sign that they moved as a horde, pouring down the northeast flank of Africa in one irresistible flow. Rather, there must have been an irregular progression of salient and then consolidation effected by the periodic mobilization of *diya* and larger kin groupings as required by the nature of the opposition.

The main opposition came from the Gallas who had preceded the Somalis as wanderers through the reaches of the Horn. Historians believe that one reason for the sustained Galla surge from the southwest into the Ethiopian highlands during the late sixteenth and seventeenth centuries was intensification of the Somali push south. In an ironic sequence of cause and effect, Galla triumphs followed by Amhara recovery and partial assimilation of the Galla elite finally closed off Somali expansion westward and thus fixed the ultimate dimensions of Somali occupation.

Gallas were not the only opponents. Parochial allegiances and, above all, the exigencies of survival in a harsh environment produced conflict among Somalis themselves, generally organized around *diya*-paying groups.

The story of Somali expansion is not only a tale of conflict. There were also some elements of cooperation and integration with prior inhabitants of the Horn and to some extent with Persian merchants who founded trading colonies at scattered locations along the coast.

But these are mere footnotes to the main tale of Somali expansion largely through the violent expulsion of predecessor peoples and the consequent establishment of a single cultural nation in continuous occupation of a vast though impoverished territory, spreading westward from the sea to the long interface with Ethiopian power.

The interface passes through three more or less distinct areas. Beginning in the north, there is the high, relatively well-watered, and regrettably brief region of sorghum cultivation running between the Somali provincial center of Harghessa and Harar, an ancient Muslim city annexed by Menelik in 1887. While part of the region is cultivated by Somali farmers, because of its abundant water during the winter dry season it is also an important gathering place for the pastoral northern clans.

South of this region is a broad sweep of dry grassland, now entirely under Ethiopian administration, called the Haud. Lacking any permanent source of water, it is habitable only during and shortly following the rainy seasons. The fact that it is used transiently makes its pasturage superior to the heavily grazed areas farther north. In the south, the Haud merges with the still larger plains of the Ogaden Desert which, in turn, roll south across the Kenya border. On the west, the plains sweep up to the Ethiopian highlands. On the east, they slip imperceptibly into the southern lowlands of Somalia.

The economic links among these areas and between them and the remainder of Somali-occupied territory are as intimate as the cultural ones. Spring and autumn see several hundred thousand herdsmen from both northern and central Somalia flooding into every part of the Haud. Somalis from the Ogaden move their herds and flocks into the Haud's periphery. After the rains, some northern clansmen, rather than returning home, go down to the wells of Ogaden clans who welcome them in reciprocity for assistance rendered by the northerners in connection with the export of livestock through the port of Berbera. Ogaden Somalis, some of whom move back and forth across the political border in their restless search for better pasture, also export livestock through the southern ports of Mogadishu and Kismayu. The latter city's meat-packing plant, built a few years ago with Russian assistance, should intensify the eastward flow of protein on the hoof.

Cultural homogeneity, a tradition of conflict with the Amharas and Gallas, and economic dependence on an open border would be sufficient in themselves to generate a powerful irredentist sentiment. Dispersal of clan families and smaller lineage groups across the surrounding international frontiers intensifies that sentiment. It is rather as if during the sixteenth century the Scottish highlands had been divided into an English-controlled shire and an independent kingdom and that the resulting border had passed right through the middle of Campbell, Macgregor, and other clan lands. If, in addition, English troops had engaged in periodic "tax collecting" expeditions against the segments of the clan-families over whom they were nominally sovereign, what highland government could have afforded to ignore the issue of "lost lands," at least while there was any real hope for their recovery?

The Colonial Partitions

The origin of existing frontiers on the Horn of Africa can easily be traced as far back as the last European scramble for African territories, which erupted on the continent like a plague in the last quarter of the nineteenth century. British, French, and Italian interests mingled competitively in and around the Horn.

The British were concerned about insuring the continuity of meat supplies from Somalia for their naval base across the gulf in Aden, a splendid port set down in the middle of rocky desolation. A modest degree of order on the Somali coast and unhindered movement along the caravan routes from the interior were essential to stable exports.

During the 1870s, these conditions were maintained by an Egyptian force that occupied the main northern ports and the interior of the Somali plateau as far west as Harar. Although initially hostile to the Egyptian presence, the British gradually recognized that occupation of the Somali coast by the army of a government over which it exercised considerable and growing influence was not inimical to their ancillary interests in the territory. In 1877, they formally recognized Egyptian jurisdiction and pressured the Italians, then ensconced around Assab, to recognize Egyptian sovereignty to the north and south.

The subsequent British occupation of Egypt in 1882 would only have enhanced the charms of an Egyptian proxy opposite Aden if the Mahdists had not, in the meantime, set about expelling the Egyptians and their British patrons from the Sudan. London concluded on behalf of Cairo that the Mahdist threat required the recall of Egyptian forces from peripheral assignments.

Gloomy intelligence from the English consul on the Somali coast followed the decision to withdraw. He predicted an outbreak of fighting between the Somalis and Gallas in the interior and an assault by the northern clans on the retiring Egyptian columns. There was, moreover, news of Mahdist stirrings among the Somalis and, to complicate matters still further, the prospect of incursions from the increasingly powerful emperor of the Abyssinians. So despite their reluctance to assume the costs of a direct presence, the British resolved to fill the imminent vacuum.

The way to a low-profile British occupation was prepared by the negotiation of treaties of protection with the elders of the Somali clans. There are two related explanations for Somali receptivity to British overtures. On the one hand, the Somalis probably were already sensitive to the growing Abyssinian power along their western flank. On the other, the agreements urged on

them by the British appeared similar in character to the contractual alliances used so extensively in Somali clan politics. In the
preamble of each treaty, the Somali party declared its purpose to
be "the maintenance of our independence, the preservation of
order, and other good and sufficient reasons." No land was
ceded. Each clan simply pledged "never to cede, sell, mortgage,
or otherwise give for occupation, save to the British Government,
any portion of the territory presently inhabited by them or being
under their control." The British, on their part, undertook to extend to the clansmen concerned and to their territories "the
gracious favour and protection of Her Majesty the Queen-
Empress."

By the end of 1884, as the Egyptians were beginning their
pullout from the interior, three British vice-consuls were established on the Somali coast, prepared—with the aid of forty
members of the Aden police, one hundred Somali coast police
who were quickly recruited and armed, and an irregular force of
armed caravan guards paid by the concerned merchants—to protect the slender national interest which had deposited them on
that very unpacific littoral.

> They were given explicit directions that their duties were those
> of British agents in a native state: they were to keep the peace,
> but not to assume powers beyond this. No grandiose schemes
> were to be entertained; expenditure was to be limited to a
> minimum, and was to be provided by the local port revenues.[3]

Almost immediately this plan for a wafer-thin, low-cost presence was threatened by a Gallic encroachment from the north.
The French, having negotiated a protectorate agreement with
that part of the Issa clan dominant in the Djibouti area, claimed
jurisdiction over the port of Djibouti in the face of British
insistence that the port fell within the sphere of its own protectorate. After much public gnashing of teeth and flexing of muscles,
the two powers were suddenly seized by a taste for conciliation.
Under the Anglo-French agreement of 1888, they recognized a
line between Djibouti and Zeila as the frontier of French Somaliland and the British Somaliland Protectorate. It was a tidy little
arrangement marred only by a dubious consistency with the protective obligations assumed by both parties in their respective
agreements with the Issas.

For the French, as for the British, the Horn's importance
stemmed from its location astride the short route to Europe. The
Italians, late-comers to the Game of Nations, found the Horn ar-

resting in its own right, there being few other places left where one could act out tardy dreams of empire. Their occupation of the Eritrean coast was facilitated by the British who, while preferring an exclusive hegemony along the Red Sea, were prepared during the early 1880s to favor a relatively weak Italy there over a considerably more puissant France.

With the coast in hand, the Italians began vigorously laying the foundations for military disaster. At first, however, everything seemed to be proceeding smoothly. They established cordial relations with King Menelik of Shoa and administered a defeat, albeit an ambiguous one, to the forces of the Tigrean emperor, Yohannes. Following the death of Yohannes in 1889, Menelik, having succeeded to the imperial throne, concluded the Treaty of Ucciali with the Italians. It recognized their sovereignty over Eritrea and, as construed by the Italians, committed Menelik to conduct his foreign relations through them, an interpretation which reduced Ethiopia to the status of a protectorate. Menelik would later claim that the Amharic version of the treaty did not contain any such commitment.

For the time being, however, he humored his Italian allies. They responded generously with loans, arms, and ammunition. Moreover, in 1890 they sponsored Ethiopian participation in the Brussels General Act which empowered Ethiopia as a Christian state to import munitions legally, thus legitimizing the active arms trade it had been carrying on for some years with French merchants. The influx of modern weapons completely destabilized the relationship between indigenous forces. They enabled Menelik first to consolidate his hold over the plateau and .then to launch his own imperial mission as well as to decimate the armies of his erstwhile superior. Fanning out in a long arc from southeast to southwest, in ten years Menelik's troops doubled the size of his kingdom. By the early 1890s, they were encroaching on the Somali lands along virtually their entire western margin. Meanwhile, the Italians, naively secure in their northern salient, were establishing, with British blessings, a second East African presence, this one on the Indian Ocean along the Benadir coast between the Juba River and the British Somaliland Protectorate.

The defeat at Adowa effectively blunted Italian encroachment on Ethiopia from the north. In the south, however, far from the center of Menelik's power, the Italians pushed steadily inward toward another rendezvous with the Ethiopians.

If the position of the Italians along the Indian Ocean coast of Somalia was largely unaffected by Adowa, the same could not be said of their British allies to the north who had until then blithely assumed that French and Italian recognition of their protectorate guaranteed its security. Reluctance to treat the Ethiopians as an important if not the leading actor in the historical drama on the Horn (occasioned no doubt by a coalition of contempt for native dynasties and wishful thinking) had survived increasing Ethiopian pressure on the northern clans who were periodically savaged by well-armed military expeditions dispatched from Harar. Nor was there any reason to believe that these were simply plundering expeditions rather than firm heralds of Ethiopian ambition to extend the empire's frontiers. As early as 1891, Menelik dispatched a letter to the British government outlining vast territorial claims. "Whilst tracing today the actual boundaries of my Empire," wrote Menelik, "I shall endeavor, if God gives me life and strength, to re-establish the ancient frontiers of Ethiopia up to Khartoum, and as far as Lake Nyanza* with all the Gallas." He included in these aspirational frontiers more than half of the British Protectorate. Assured by the Italians that Menelik was safely ensconced under their thumb, the British ignored what must have seemed to them the ravings of another deranged Abyssinian potentate. The emperor Tewodros had displayed a similar verbal audacity, but when it came to the test of arms, his boasts had proved as empty as his armory. So why worry?

Adowa provided an abrupt answer. It was accompanied by the multiplication of Ethiopian belligerents along the protectorate's borders. Ras Makonnen, Menelik's representative in Harar and the father of Haile Selassie, threatened to assert by force Ethiopian jurisdiction over the land well east of the line acknowledged in an 1894 Anglo-Italian protocol as defining the frontier between their respective domains.

With events moving rapidly toward a violent climax, the British decided to subordinate racial pride to a crassly economic calculus of the national interest. If, as appeared likely, the emperor could himself maintain the requisite degree of order within his possessions, there was no need for a costly armed struggle over who owned exactly which piece of land in which the British had such marginal interests.

Less then twelve months after Adowa, the British government dispatched a special envoy, Rennell Rodd, to settle all outstanding issues between Britain and the now clearly formidable Menelik. Rodd knew that, with respect to the matter of the protectorate's

* Lake Victoria.

border, he would be negotiating from a position of pathetic weakness, for not only was his government extremely reluctant to pursue its claims by military means; in addition, it was anxious for Ethiopian support of Britain's campaign against the Sudanese Mahdists. Furthermore, Rodd was preceded by a French envoy who had gracefully sustained the traditional cordiality of Franco-Ethiopian relations by agreeing to redraw the frontier of the French enclave to a point no greater than one hundred kilometers inland, a very considerable retrenchment of French claims.

Within the limitations of his hand, Rodd played his cards effectively. He convinced Menelik to drop an initial claim to the entire British Protectorate; the precise boundary limitation was left to subsequent negotiations between Rodd and Ras Makonnen. But an annexed stipulation that such Somali clansmen who, as a result of any adjustment of boundaries, might eventually become Ethiopian subjects were to be well treated and assured of "orderly government" foreshadowed some measure of territorial concession by the British. After prolonged negotiations in Harar, Rodd and Makonnen managed the following compromise: Britain abandoned its claims to some 67,000 square miles of land in and immediately north of the Haud; Ethiopia, for its part, recognized British suzerainty to a line 50 miles west of the main interior Somali town, Harghessa.

In what appears to have been a display of syntactical wiliness, Rodd secured Ethiopian *recognition* of British authority while describing Britain's concession as a mere withdrawal of claims to act on behalf of peoples occupying the westernmost part of the Somali Plateau. Under the agreement, Britain neither formally ceded the land in question nor recognized Ethiopia as the new governing authority. Hence, there was no formal conflict with the Anglo-Italian protocol of 1894. The treaties of protection fared less well. Britain had implicitly promised to protect the independence of the clans. Independence was meaningless if it could be exercised only by relinquishing control of land essential to the clan's economy. From Lord Salisbury's Olympian perspective, this was a matter of little consequence. "[He] was not much preoccupied about Abyssinian encroachments in Somaliland," Rodd wrote following an interview with that distinguished personage.

The handful of colonial servants responsible for the administration of the protectorate were rather more agitated. But they drew solace from the treaty's provision that Somalis would be free to use wells and graze their cattle on both sides of the frontier without hindrance and also from two assumptions: that there would be a very low order of permanent Somali settlement in the relinquished land and, second, that the Ethiopians would not attempt to establish themselves in the area as the effective administering authority. The former assumption was gradually dispelled, on the one hand, by a rapid increase in the settlement of Somali nomads for purposes of sorghum cultivation and, on the other, by a continuing growth in the use of the Haud by clans unable to maintain their herds in the eroded, overgrazed north. The second assumption subsided at a rate which varied for different parts of the relinquished area largely as a function of soil fertility. As far as merely pastoral land was concerned, for several decades "administration" continued to be indistinguishable from sporadic extortionate intrusions by Ethiopian raiding parties. The thinness of their administrative presence postponed until 1934 a felt need on the Ethiopians' part for on-the-ground demarcation of the border. And it was only then that the Somali nomads discovered the contents of the agreement which, whatever its formal terms, remitted the Somali clans to the de facto authority of a hostile Christian empire, a consequence clearly envisioned by both parties to the treaty.

Cultivated or cultivable land drew earlier and more-sustained attention from the Ethiopian authorities. Frustrated by Somali resistance to exactions of grain and meat designed for the support of Ethiopian officials and occupying troops, beginning around 1918 they began to settle Galla and Amhara farmers in areas of Somali cultivation and pasturage.

Rodd, astride his mule on the road to Harar for the second phase of his negotiations, passed his Italian counterpart, Major Nerazzini, bound for Addis in pursuit of a southern border agreement. By all accounts, Nerazzini's negotiations with Menelik were concluded amicably, but with exceeding informality. Apparently, they simply drew an agreed line on two copies of a map. Nothing was put in writing. The maps were eventually lost. And the only surviving direct evidence of their agreement is Nerazzini's report to his government in which he claimed Ethiopian recognition of an Italian zone of absolute possession "from the intersection of our frontier with that of British Somaliland, . . . parallel to the coast extending about 180 miles inland," a distance considerably short of Italian claims before Adowa. Since Rodd was engaged with Makonnen in fixing the boundaries of British Somaliland at the very time Nerazzini was negotiating with Menelik, one could have anticipated discordant interpretations of their agreement.

The expectation was quickly fulfilled. In 1908, coincident with the payment of three million Italian lira to Menelik, the parties agreed on a clarification which at least the Italians believed confirmed Nerazzini's version of his agreement with Menelik. Thereafter, as Italian power grew alongside its imperial interests in southern Somalia, the incentive to further clarification correspondingly receded, to vanish altogether with the rise of a fascist dictator determined to erect an Italian empire on the Horn of Africa.

All in all, 1897 was a banner year for Ethiopia. Each of its European colonial neighbors had sharply contracted its territorial claims and manifested a pressing desire for Ethiopian friendship. It was now evident that friendship would be given only on terms of absolute equality. There would be no more nonsense about protectorates. A great year for Ethiopians; a black one for Somalis, although, since they were neither consulted before nor informed after the agreements, it was years before they would appreciate what had happened.

From 1897 to 1935, the only significant change in the political frontiers dividing the Somali people occurred in the south. Under the terms of an 1891 agreement, the Italians recognized a zone of British influence from the southern border of Kenya all the way north to the Juba River which flows through the Ogaden and southern Somalia to the sea. During the first four years after the conclusion of that accord, the port of Kismayu and the surrounding territory was left in the hands of the Imperial British East Africa Company. The company might as well have assumed responsibility for the domestication of a spitting cobra. Relations with the fractious local clans came to a pustulent head in 1895 with a savage battle in and around the town followed by the withdrawal of the Somali population to the countryside. Before the year's end, the company gave its concession up as a thoroughly bad show. The British government, assuming control, proclaimed a protectorate over "Jubaland."

The change in the administration did not alter the belligerent temper of the Jubaland clans. A costly punitive expedition quickly dispatched to the interior to confirm British authority, though unable to force a battle, was repeatedly harassed and finally returned to the coast with little if any accomplishment to its credit. It seemed likely that more such expeditions would be required. And they were.

Jubaland, embracing what is today southern Somalia and the northeast district of Kenya, had as little material value to the British as their possessions in the northern Horn. But administration has its own logic, which is order. Order meant action to reduce three kinds of conflicts: between Somali clans, between Somalis and Gallas, and between Somalis and the plundering expeditions which sallied periodically out of the Ethiopian highlands. To that end, the British gradually extended their effective authority farther and farther into the interior. They exercised their extended reach to terminate the 900-year march of the Somali nation down the coast of East Africa. Confronted by British power, the Somalis were forced to accept the Tana River as their southern frontier. There it has remained.

The Anglo-Italian alliance in the First World War created a respectable rationale for Britain to reduce its unrewarding obligations north of the Tana River. Among the inducements for Italian participation in the war was a British commitment in 1915, under the secret Treaty of London, that if Great Britain increased its colonial territory in Africa at the expense of Germany, the British government would agree in principle that Italy might claim some equitable compensation. Having through acquisition of the German colony of Tanganyika satisfied the condition precedent, Britain concluded a convention ceding 33,000 square miles of Jubaland to Italy. Implementation of the convention was postponed by five years of wrangling over unrelated conditions of the postwar settlement. During the interregnum, several members of Parliament thought to question the compatibility of the transfer with "the principle of self-determination" and, more generally, with the welfare of Jubaland's inhabitants. The foreign secretary disposed of such cavils by noting that "no condition as to the consent of the inhabitants was made in the Treaty of London." On June 29, 1925, the transfer to Italy was completed.

Although L. S. Amery, a government spokesman in the House of Commons, had insisted that "the reason for the cession of the territory as a whole is to keep these tribes together as a single unit, and give them the full use of their natural grazing ground" and the Earl of Onslow had assured such lords as were present, *compos mentis,* and awake that "the line has been drawn as closely as possible in accordance with racial divisions," in fact, thousands of square miles inhabited by tens of thousands of Somalis—the current population approaches a quarter of a million— were sliced off the main body of Somali territory, thus planting additional seeds of conflict.

No account of Somali modern history would be complete without some reference to the unsuccessful war of independence organized and led by Sheikh Mohammed Abdille Hassan. To the

British, held at bay for twenty years by his tactical brilliance and political virtuosity, he was the "Mad Mullah," as if no sane Somali could object to such a benevolent protector. Sheikh Mohammed, after traveling to Mecca and joining an ascetic, reforming religious order, returned to the northern Somali coast around 1897 to teach, preach, and with messianic zeal exhort his countrymen to return to the strict path of Muslim devotion. Whether they emerged in Roman Palestine, British Somaliland, or any other place under alien domination, messianic figures of this type posed threats to law and order. The sheikh was no exception. He would have been a troublemaker under any circumstances. Under the actual circumstances of his emergence, including the inspirational example of the Mahdists' holy struggle for freedom in the Sudan, the activities of Christian missionaries operating along the coast under the protection of colonial governments, and, above all, British supineness in the face of Ethiopian encroachment on Somali lands, the trouble he would make was bound to be large.

At the turn of the century, this extraordinary man set about liberating his people from "infidel" domination. He soon announced his intention with the sure eloquence which helped make him a myth in his own lifetime. In a letter addressed to the English people, he wrote:

> If the country (Somaliland) was cultivated, or contained houses or property it would be worth your while to fight. . . . If you want wood or stone you can get them in plenty. There are also many ant heaps. The sun is very hot. All you can get from me is war, nothing else.[4]

Such gorgeous arrogance is reminiscent of a neighboring reformer, Tewodros, who announced defiantly:

> I know the tactics of European governments when they desire to acquire an eastern state. First they send out missionaries, then consuls to support the missionaries, then battalions to support the consuls. I am not a Rajah of Hindustan to be made a mock of in that way. I prefer to have to deal with the battalions straight away![5]

Sheikh Mohammed had to deal not only with British battalions but with Ethiopian ones as well. His aim was liberation of all Somalis from every alien power. He appealed for support not merely to the Darods, his patrilineal clan, and to the Dublahantes, his mother's people, but to all Somalis. He was, in short, the first truly nationalist leader.

Ancient divisions branded on Somali society by the ruthless conditions of survival could not be erased overnight. Nor for that matter in twenty years. Nor by any single man. The determined divisiveness of his people, perhaps as much as the Ethiopian-British alliance, the coastal blockade on arms, and the troops and even planes thrown into the struggle by the British, finally defeated him. But not before he awakened and nourished the idea that beyond the ties of lineage and blood-contract there were bonds among all Somalis which in the modern world must take precedence, for narrower loyalties lead only to submission. His call to the nation, his appeal to moral regeneration, and his vision of liberation, captured in the lines of his abundant poetry, quickly passed into the vital oral tradition which linked a trader in Djibouti to a nomad in the Ogaden. So though he was defeated, he did not entirely fail.

The defeat and death of Sheikh Mohammed, coming as it did at the end of an exhausting European war in which the three European powers on the Horn had been allied, seemed to promise an extended period of tranquility. There was no figure of comparable appeal and ability to marshal internal dissidents; the state actors were nominally satisfied with existing boundaries. And though there remained some uncertainty about the precise location of the frontier between Italian Somaliland and Ethiopia, uncertainty seemed to function within a rather narrow order of magnitude. The whole place seemed nothing short of a political Elysium but for one small difficulty: the Italian Right had neither forgotten Adowa nor surrendered its dreams of empire, dreams that may easily have been sharpened by the niggardly compensation awarded to Italy for its dreadful losses incurred during the World War.

By the late 1920s, the colonial authorities in Mogadishu, following up earlier political and economic infiltration, were conducting covert military probes of parts of the Ogaden farther inland than any interpretation of the 1897 and 1908 agreements could justify.

Several prominent religious leaders across the border had now been won to the Italian cause by generous gifts. Irregular Somali groups, who could be disclaimed conveniently as bandits, were also recruited and provided with arms to stir up trouble in the area. Thus in the Mustahil region, Ololdin, the forceful Ajuran sultan, was paid and armed by the Italians to attack the

Ethiopian tribute-gathering expeditions whose arbitrary activities constituted virtually all that there was at this time in the way of Ethiopian administration.[6]

The Emperor, at the center of his Byzantine web in Addis, took note of the Italian encroachments and, although he made no official protests, maneuvered to resist them. He cultivated the support of Ogaden Somalis by offering guns and ammunition to those who expressed hostility to the Italians. And lest the Italians think that Ethiopia had lost its sting, he sent out still larger and better-armed tribute-gathering parties to points farther and farther east.

But he was playing a losing game. In currying favor with the clans, as with armaments and great-power diplomacy, the Italians had irremedial advantages. They were not historic enemies of the Somalis. They could offer far more in the way of money and guns. And, although as Christian as the Amharas, they seemed a good deal more respectful of Muslim sentiment. Tribute was not their game. The focus for exploitation and Italian settlement was the inter-river area nearer the Indian Ocean coast. From the Ogaden tribes and other Somali nomads they sought military support. And for the most part they got it. There were 40,000 Somali troops in the Italian army which in 1935, after a carefully orchestrated "border incident" deep inside the Ogaden, marched into the highlands and occupied Addis, thus launching the Italian East African empire.

Il Duce's forces went from victory to victory. British Somaliland was next on the agenda. On August 4, 1940, Italy threw in entire divisions supported by tanks and artillery against a mixed handful of lightly armed defenders. After seven days of bitter combat, British survivors were evacuated to Aden through the port of Berbera. For the first time, the great majority of Somalis were united within a single political enterprise. Only Djibouti and the Northern Frontier District of Kenya were excluded. And the latter was added seven months later when the British blasted their way back into Somalia and rolled up the Italian army all the way to the farthest extremities of Ethiopia. French Somaliland remained, as ever, aloof. Its Vichy master successfully endured a British blockade until late 1942 when, with the prospect of German victory annulled, one of his unit commanders withdrew across the border, received DeGaulle's imprimatur, and marched back in for the glory of Free France. *Plus ça change, plus c'est la même chose.*

Occupation by a single power coincided with a quickening of

the nationalist ideal illuminated by Sheikh Mohammed Abdille Hassan. He had fought his war in the countryside. But in Somalia after his death, as in most other parts of Africa, the city became the focus of nationalist activity. There, thrown together with men and women unrelated by ties of blood, freed of the economic and martial imperatives which in the country compelled parochial attachments, and confronted by a people alien in color and culture, Somalis discovered the possibility and potential efficacy of new and larger alliances based on the common denominators of language, religion, and a shared oppression. The southern towns and cities, their economies stimulated by preparations for war, grew throughout the 1930s. Italian defeat brought economic depression. Demobilized Somali troops further swelled the urban population. In Eritrea, unemployment and the deflation of Italian prestige had released a subterranean current of hostility. Somalia was no different. With the approval of the British administration, a group of young activists founded the first Somali political movement, the Somali Youth Club. It pledged opposition to any renewal of Italian hegemony.

Set against the favorable omens of a unified administration and incipient political organization was the triumphant return from exile of Haile Selassie. The ageless perfection of imperial dignity, so trim, graceful, and supremely cool that physically larger men seemed gross by comparison, he began a relentless campaign for the consolidation of personal power and the expansion of the Ethiopian state. The anointed martyr of fascist aggression, as wily as ever, cloaked his own ambitions in the rhetoric of liberation and restoration. Shortly before his return, he announced these themes in leaflets showered over Eritrea by the Royal Air Force. "I have come," he proclaimed, "to restore the independence of my country, including Eritrea and the Benadir [the old name for the coast of southern Somalia] whose people will henceforth dwell under the shade of the Ethiopian flag." In a later memorandum to the United Nations, his government would claim that "prior to the race of the European powers to divide up the continent of Africa, Ethiopia included an extensive coastline along the Red Sea and Indian Ocean." A thrilling piece of mendacity, of course, yet thoroughly consistent with universal canons of diplomatic propriety. What matters to most governments almost all the time is results. Haile Selassie had few rivals in the ability to obtain them.

The British, having betrayed the Somalis for reasons of state in 1897, had a solid precedent for doing it again. And England is, after all, a common-law country where precedent really counts. John Drysdale, distinguished chronicler of the Somali-Ethiopian dispute, believed that Anthony Eden foreshadowed the renewed fragmentation of the Somali nation in a major policy statement to the House of Commons in early February, 1941:

> His Majesty's Government would welcome the reappearance of an Ethiopian State and recognize the claim of the Emperor Haile Selassie to the throne. . . . [His Majesty's Government] reaffirm that they have themselves no territorial ambitions in Abyssinia.

Recognition of Selassie's claim to the throne was consistent with the overall policy of restoring the status quo wherever it had enhanced British power, wealth, and influence: a king in Greece, an emperor in Ethiopia, His Majesty's government in Burma, Malaya, Hong Kong, and every other corner of the empire on which the sun would nevertheless soon set. That was to be expected. The denial of territorial ambitions was a nice gesture, calculated to heighten the distinction between Nazi aggression and Allied response. Moreover, the British had never really worked up a consistent interest in Ethiopia, even at the high-water mark of European frenzy over colonial opportunities in Africa. There were enough other places for the provision of outdoor relief to the younger sons of the gentry.

Surrender of Somali-occupied land was not the logical converse either of this self-denying ordinance or of the "reappearance" of an independent Ethiopian state. That state had existed in one form or another for 2,000 years. From the High Middle Ages until Menelik's Western-armed essays in black imperialism, its writ had not run in any Somali-occupied territory, although from time to time it might have succeeded in exacting a payment of tribute from one or another nomadic group. What Menelik had taken by force or the threat thereof, the Italians had taken back in kind. Britain had recognized each successive act of conquest. Since Britain and most other Western states had extended de jure recognition to Italian absorption of Ethiopia before the outbreak of World War II, no principle of prewar legitimacy required re-establishment of the Ethiopian state *within the particular boundaries hacked out by Menelik.* And if the Somalis or the Eritreans were not deemed ready to manage their own affairs and the British were unwilling to acquire title to the border territories wrenched by Italy from Ethiopian hands, there was the alternative of a trusteeship, whether administered by the United Kingdom, a group of United Nations members, or the United Nations itself.

This was logically possible. It just was not what His Brittanic Majesty's government had in mind. In 1942, it responded to the Emperor's tireless exhortations by concluding an agreement with him restoring full sovereignty to Ethiopia and confirming the prewar boundary between Ethiopia and the British Protectorate; the agreement was, however, qualified by an associated military convention granting Britain temporary administrative authority in the Ogaden and the Reserved Area. The former was defined as stretching from the northeast corner of Kenya to the southern boundary of British Somaliland; for the sake of administrative convenience, it would continue to be administered as part of Italian Somaliland. The Reserved Area included the Haud and the grain-producing areas to the west of the protectorate, in short, most of the territory subject to the 1897 agreement.

Following the convention's renewal in 1944, the Emperor began to press hard for the rapid withdrawal of British authority. In the meantime, sympathy for the Somalis was percolating up from British officers on the Horn to rarified levels of political decision. Drysdale writes that, as early as 1943, the men in the field had come to appreciate the humanitarian case for a unified administration responsive to the problems of a people

> who live precarious lives from one long drought to another; people who must follow the rains in one season and orbit around wells in the next; people who have their own unique system of social security and administration of justice. These people also need, from time to time, the intervention and assistance of a modern centralised government to regulate and control water and pasture; to extract underground water intelligently so that it does not upset the delicate balance between migrations, pasture and waters; to bolster their judicial system which artificial boundaries destroy; and to restore equilibrium between clans by a policy of disarmament.[7]

Their arguments finally had consequential impact in Whitehall. When, in 1946, the Big Four took up the question of Italian Somaliland, the British foreign secretary, Ernest Bevin, proposed that

> British Somaliland, Italian Somaliland, and the adjacent part of Ethiopia, if Ethiopia agreed, should be lumped together as a trust territory, so that the nomads should lead their frugal existence with the least possible hindrance and there might be a real chance of a decent economic life, as understood in that territory.

The proposal, however well intentioned, was intrinsically flawed by the provisions requiring Ethiopian agreement and proposing a British trustee. The former could not be satisfied. The latter, although it was not put forward as an essential condition, nevertheless encouraged perception of the plan as a stratagem for British imperial expansion.

Unable to satisfy the conditions for its omnibus plan, Britain then attempted a bilateral deal with the Ethiopians who were offered the port of Zeila in the extreme north of the protectorate in return for cession to Britain of the Ogaden and the Haud. Had the British succeeded, the broader Somali unity they had urged on their allies would have been consummated in 1960 when the protectorate and Italian Somaliland achieved independence and then immediately merged.

But like Britain's earlier initiative, it was no sooner launched than it sank. The French, exercising rights under a 1906 agreement with the United Kingdom, vetoed the proposal for construction of a rail link from Ethiopia to Zeila which would, of course, have reduced the commerce of Djibouti. That, however, was a mere footnote to the inevitable disinterest of the Ethiopians once it became evident that they would acquire direct access to the sea through hegemony in Eritrea.

After withdrawing from the Ogaden in 1948 but retaining certain residual rights of supervision over Somali clans pasturing transiently in the Haud, the British government made a last futile effort to fulfill its original protective obligation by offering to purchase the southern and western grazing areas of the protectorate clans. Haile Selassie rejected the idea out of hand.

Somali nationalism raced unsuccessfully to catch up with the irretrievable flow of events. Its leading institutional expression, the Somali Youth Club, opened at Mogadishu in May, 1943, with thirteen members, including several prominent religious leaders, representing all of the main clan groups. They were united by a desire to transcend clan rivalries and to forge a political nation which would be both the embodiment of Islamic values and a vehicle of secular progress. This marriage of tradition and modernity, consummated in the tolerant political atmosphere maintained by the British administration, appealed strongly to younger, educated Somalis then beginning to multiply in the civil service and also in the gendarmerie whose British senior officers employed a conscious policy of clan-mixing at every level and promoted a code of translineage loyalty. Within three years, the original club had acquired what British officials estimated to be no less than 25,000 affiliates scattered throughout

British-occupied territory. Already a de facto political institution, in 1947 it adopted the corresponding forms by changing its name to the Somali Youth League (SYL) and announcing a program emphasizing promotion of Somali unity, repudiation of clan distinctions, the spread of modern education, and development of a written script for the Somali language. As a prelude to full independence, it urged a ten-year trusteeship under Big Four administration.

Despite compelling evidence of widespread public support for the SYL and equally extensive hostility to the Italians, Britain joined the United States and France in supporting an Italian trusteeship, the result urged by Italy's newly elected Christian Democratic government. Russia, having witnessed the defeat of its favorite party in the 1948 Italian elections, found categorical merit in the idea of a trusteeship by the Big Four. And so, under the rule of unanimity, the Somali issue was shuffled over to the United Nations General Assembly, where a majority, as ever in search of the golden mean, decided in favor of Italian administration but only for ten years and under close United Nations supervision. That stout champion of Somali self-determination, Emperor Haile Selassie, responded with a condemnatory cable to the United Nations Secretary-General: "In overriding the principles of self-determination of peoples so clearly expressed by the Somali people . . . the fourth General Assembly failed in its responsibility for reaching decisions urgently required in the interests of peace and justice. . . ."

Particularly in light of the fact that in reaching this result the General Assembly had modified a Bevin-Sforza "compromise" calling for an Italian trusteeship to last an unspecified period, SYL demonstrations at home and diplomacy abroad could be credited with a partial victory. The sense of achievement in the case of Italian Somalia could only be heightened by the string of disasters on the Ethiopian front. They were epitomized by the 1948 massacre of SYL supporters in Jijiga following Britain's agreement to withdraw from the Ogaden. As described by John Drysdale with that legal punctilio so characteristic of British colonial officials:

> . . . Major Demeka, the governor-designate of the Ogaden Province, requested the British military administration, which was still in charge, to remove the SYL flag flying from party headquarters. It had been run up to give offense to the Ethiopians and was in fact illegal. As the leaders refused to pull down their flag, the police brought it down with a machine gun mounted on an armoured car. Disturbances followed, during

which a policeman was killed and another wounded by the ex-
plosion of a hand grenade thrown from the roof of the SYL
headquarters. The police opened fire on the crowd, killing
twenty-five of them and that was the end of the final act of defiance by the SYL before it was proscribed, as are all political
parties in Ethiopia. Thus, after thirteen years, Ethiopian administration of Jijiga and Dagabur was resumed. Ethiopian
district governors were then dispatched to [the main district
towns], and the eastern part of the Ogaden was administered
by Ethiopian officials on September 23, 1948, for the first time
in its history.[8]

In the words of Ian Lewis's epitaph for the Ogaden Somalis,
"The tribute-gathering sorties which Ras Makonnen had sent out
from Harar and Jigjiga at the turn of the century, which had
created a basis for Ethiopia's pretensions to sovereignty over the
Ogaden, had at last borne fruit."[9]

The turbulence of the late 1940s was followed in the south by
ten relatively pacific years. They began somewhat inauspiciously
with the establishment of an Italian Trusteeship Administration
inclined neither to forgive nor to forget its opponents. Sympto-
matic was the allocation of pains and indulgences within the
former gendarmerie. Somalis suspected of infection by Anglo-
philia or nationalism — primarily SYL members — were weeded
out of promotion courses and either sacked or banished to remote bush posts. Fortunately for the trust territory's tranquility,
an evident desire to satisfy the obligations of a trustee quickly
dispelled the initial spirit of revanche.

Even while applying the *lex talionis,* Italian officials had initiated programs for the repair and enlargement of the territory's
physical infrastructure, for the development of agriculture, and
for the promotion of basic education and technical training. Progress accelerated as Italian officials lost either the arrogance or
paranoia which had prompted their initial repression.

As early as 1956, the Italian administration replaced all expa-
triate district and provincial commissioners with Somalis. Two
years later, Col. Mohammed Abshir assumed command of the
Somali police force.

The administration managed a parallel transfer of political
authority. Municipal elections in 1954 were followed two years
later by elections to form a parliamentary government with
power over domestic legislation, subject to veto by the head of the
administration. Of sixty available seats, the SYL won forty-three;
the next largest party won only thirteen. Four years later, the league
enlarged its already huge majority and was then authorized to form
the first government of an independent Somali state.

Events moved more erratically in the British Somaliland Protectorate. Prior to 1955, the festering situation in the transborder grazing lands absorbed indigenous concern. Ethiopian officials worked ceaselessly to undermine the continued British presence. Conflict revolved around the issue of who should be regarded as an Ethiopian subject. While the Emperor had reaffirmed the provisions of the 1897 agreement concerning free movement, he was clearly determined to enhance the charms of at least nominal identification with Ethiopia. To that end, his officials violated the nomads' democratic tradition by appointing some of their number as, in effect, chiefs to serve as intermediaries with Ethiopian authorities. These appointed officials were paid by the Ethiopian government. Perhaps because British officials in the field struggled to preserve Somali rights, political activity within the protectorate seemed narcotized until suddenly, at the end of 1954, quite without warning to the Somalis, the British government concluded a new agreement with the Emperor ceding the last vestige of its authority in the Reserved Area. In return, the Ethiopian government reaffirmed once again the right of British-protected clans to graze and water in the traditional manner.

Somalis in the protectorate had apparently clung to the hope of ultimate diplomatic action by the British to re-create a unified administration or at least to strengthen the safeguards for cross-border migration. Now, obviously feeling the victims of an ultimate betrayal (when, in fact, the British had one more stiletto to plant in the Somali back), they staged mass demonstrations throughout the protectorate demanding recovery of the lost territories and, for the first time, independence. As a step toward the former objective, they asked the British authorities to sponsor resolutions in the United Nations General Assembly calling for an advisory opinion of the International Court of justice on the status of the ceded territories, in effect on the power of the United Kingdom to cede them.

Apparently fearing the precedential consequence of any external appreciation of agreements with or concerning its colonies and protectorates, the British government refused. A Colonial Office publication defended the decision on the grounds that "the Protectorate having been established in 1887, HMG [Her Majesty's Government] had been fully entitled to conclude the Treaty of 1897." This was, of course, one of the issues which the Somalis wished to submit for adjudication.

The only British concession to Somali feeling concerning the lost grazing areas was the foredoomed offer mentioned above to purchase the land. In addition to failing on that score, the British were unable to moderate Ethiopian efforts to extract acknowledgment of Ethiopian nationality and deference to Ethiopian authority from the nomadic Somali clans.

Failure in Addis coincided with British announcement of a program looking toward rapid achievement of internal self-government in the protectorate and of sympathy for the aspiration to union with Italian Somalia. Final cession of British authority in the transborder grazing lands undoubtedly shredded British prestige and hence the authority of the protectorate administration. As in many other colonial settings, its rule had rested on the acquiescence of the governed induced by their political fragmentation, their absorption in parochial matters left untouched by the administration, and undoubtedly their assumption that behind all the bumptious self-confidence of the handful of administrators there lay real power which could be mobilized against the Somalis and which could also protect their interests from more-dangerous predators. The unequivocal loss of the grazing lands destroyed the three pillars of colonial bluff: it created an issue transcending clan lines, it directly affected the lives of individual Somalis, and it revealed the emptiness of the protector's promises. Either he was weak or he had betrayed his clients. In either event, he was useless. With the basis for acquiescence destroyed, the British could either leave or fight.

In Kenya they had fought for a while. It had 40,000 white settlers, British investments worth millions of pounds, a first-class port, and a rich agriculture. Yet even Kenya proved too expensive once the native population achieved a modest degree of political mobilization. The protectorate had no settlers, no investment, no wealth, and a port incomparably inferior to Aden and Mombasa. It was as poor as the day the British had arrived. Clearly it was time to leave.

The administration set about frantically creating the apparatus of a parliamentary government and indigenous administration. Scholarships and training courses rained down on the population. There was a little flurry of public works activity. It must have been like a manic exercise in spring cleaning after years of winter.

Notes

For information on Somali history and society the author is particularly indebted to books by John Drysdale and Ian Lewis: Drysdale, *The Somali Dispute* (New York: Praeger, 1964) ; Lewis, *The Modern History of Somaliland* (New York:

Praeger, 1965). Two other valuable sources are Irving Kaplan *et al, Area Handbook for Somalia* (Washington, D.C.: American University Foreign Area Studies, 1970) and S. Touval, *Somali Nationalism* (Cambridge: Harvard University Press, 1963).

1. Drysdale, p. 10.

2. Lewis, p. 11.

3. *Ibid.*

4. Quoted in Drysdale, p. 32.

5. Quoted in Greenfield, p. 70.

6. Lewis, p. 108.

7. Drysdale, p. 62.

8. *Ibid,* pp. 70-1.

9. Lewis, p. 130.

Independence: A Partial Victory 5

On June 26, 1960, the British Somaliland Protectorate achieved full independence. Five days later, when the Italian Trust Territory of Somalia emerged from its cocoon as an independent state, the two entities united pursuant to accords negotiated during the preceding months. The accords established a unitary republic with northern and southern regions. On the flag of the new state there was a five-pointed star. Those points, a government spokesman announced and the constitution affirmed, represented the five fragments of the Somali nation created by the colonial impact on the Horn. Fusion of the protectorate and the trust territory was the first step toward the consummation of national unity. The Somalis were determined that it would not be the last.

Freedom and its Discontents

The Somali Democratic Republic launched its pursuit of national unity from a miserably weak economic base. Bananas and cattle were the only two exports of any substantial value. The foreign exchange they earned was insufficient to permit infrastructure maintenance and to satisfy existing consumer demand, much less to support any program of military and economic development. Government revenues, essentially import and export duties, were equally inadequate despite the extremely narrow range of public service activities. Mogadishu, for instance, had no potable water until the end of the decade.

The new government was therefore compelled to live off foreign aid. Britain promised £1.5 million during the first year of independence with further grants to be negotiated. Italy offered an annual grant of £3 million. Both sums represented a mélange of budgetary support, technical assistance, and development projects.

In the sphere of development, Britain and Italy were quickly joined by a host of other donors, including the United States, West Germany, the USSR, Czechoslovakia, the People's Republic of China, the United Arab Republic, the United Nations Development Programme, and other specialized agencies of the United Nations.

The donors piled proposals and to a lesser extent money on a structure of government characterized by political sophistication at the highest levels and managerial incompetence nearly everywhere. Flaunting the most atrocious characteristics of the Italian bureaucracy from which southern-born officials drew their inspiration, the civil service wallowed in a morass of indolence and red tape. Northerners who migrated to Mogadishu often complained bitterly about deviations from the starchy efficiency they imputed to British colonial officials. But either because they were too few or the atmosphere too seductive, the northerners seemed unable to affect the overall tone of public life in this miniature Rome on the Indian Ocean. The single clear exception to the general standard of public service was the 5,000-man police force which combined ordinary police functions with intelligence and paramilitary operations designed to prevent interclan violence and to safeguard the border. Foreign observers were pretty much uniform in the belief that its efficiency, vigor, and honesty compared favorably with similar units in other parts of the globe.

It is uncertain whether the bureaucratic slough of inefficiency had a great deal of economic consequence. There was, of course, no effective planning mechanism, no basis for project selection and integration. And most of the various donors were far too busy ignoring each other and scratching for an edge in the local influence game to attempt any coordination themselves. Still, the country needed so much of everything that there was little risk of wasteful duplication. There were, however, disastrous failures of coordination: a milk-bottling plant without milk; a magnificent hospital without technicians, maintenance crews, or doctors; and so on.

Even if every failure of conception, coordination, and execution in the first few years of independence had been averted — something that happens in no country whatever its stage of development or form of government — the economic and social consequences would, I think, have been marginal to the country's extreme poverty, a poverty of natural resources, technology, basic education, health, nutrition, infrastructure, plant, and equipment. Not different or better projects but rather a totally different model of development emphasizing austere administrative expenditure, severe restrictions on private affluence, and the mobilization of all local and donated resources to raise the subsistence levels among the eighty percent of the population struggling to survive from one season of rains to another conceivably might have altered the face of poverty in Somalia. It would have taken that model plus a government with the prestige, power, competence, and commitment required to make that model work.

The government which assumed office in 1960 had none of these qualities. To some degree it serviced, to some degree it simply fed on the laissez faire economy inherited from the colonial era. It interfered hardly at all with the pre-existing pattern of rural and urban life. It acted, in short, like most postcolonial governments. Because it started from a very low economic base, the country was far poorer after half a decade of independence than countries like Kenya or Ghana which had launched themselves from a much higher base. Because its government effectively represented the tense balance of forces in an unusually egalitarian social system, Somalia seemed freer, less coercive than most of its counterparts. And this was what many Westerners who lived in Somalia during the early 1960s found so engaging, this and the system of private generosity — part Islamic, in large part the triumph of clan over class — which seemed to dull the sharper edges of privation. At the same time, there was a sense both among foreign observers and the narrow wedge of modernizers — students, a few professionals, recent graduates in the civil service, the police, and the army — that economically the society was having difficulty moving off dead center, that it was stagnant, falling further behind the wealthier countries of Africa. And some, certainly some of the students, began to wonder whether a political system organized like this one could ever effect the necessary changes. It is, of course, hard to accept, even to contemplate the possibility that the inherent obstacles to full-scale modernization may be insuperable.

If an outsider had concluded — on the basis of the casual flow of petitioners to the government compound, the vigorous debates in the National Assembly, the spirited political rallies, the incessant political chatter on the streets and in the coffee-houses, and the total absence of that telltale guarded sibilance of speech familiar to travelers through any police state — that Somalia was a real democracy, he would have been right. But it was, nevertheless, a rather special kind of democracy.

Despite the growth of nationalist sentiment, for the average Somali, when it came to domestic politics, kinship remained the basis of selection. The relevant kinship group might be defined more broadly than it had been in the past when there was rarely a means for marshaling entire clans or clan-families, which, in the case of the largest ones, might have hundreds of thousands of members. Electoral competition and the related struggle for jobs and development funds now lent significance to these more extended relationships. There were enough cabinet posts to assure balanced representation only among the larger lineage groups.

Americans can attest that there is nothing very special about ethnic politics. It is all a matter of degree. In Somalia, the degree was on the extreme side.

Ethnic politics of any kind tends to subordinate the electoral significance of a candidate's program and personal qualities. Somali ethnic politics heightened this tendency because it mirrored the traditional hierarchies of prestige within the clans: older men in general, elders from particularly distinguished families, men with a reputation for religiosity (which could be fostered by a pilgrimage to Mecca), and wealthy men — both of the last two more likely to be older than younger. The importance of these qualities further limited the pool of potentially successful candidates and thus effected the further subordination of program and personal qualities relevant to the formulation and implementation of a development program. Ethnic politics also introduced an element of gerontocracy into the political system, again a question of degree but one which is fairly consequential in an impoverished, ancient society experiencing the traumas of modernization.

All of these sociological dimensions of the political process reinforced the natural tendency of democratic politics to prevent the articulation and implementation of a coherent policy of social transformation and to encourage an emphasis on the division of spoils within the existing societal parameters. As long as there are enough goods to satisfy the expectations of all major groups, this kind of arrangement is likely to be stable. In developing, and particularly in recently decolonized, countries, that essential condition of stability is difficult to find. Where there is no large industrial-commercial sector, government employment is the primary source of affluence, power, and status. There are never enough desirable jobs for the accumulating layers of university graduates.

Aggravating these tensions is the inevitable disillusion which follows the consummation of independence. The oppressor leaves, yet so many of those problems of poverty and inequality, of personal and group animosity, once attributed (in many cases justly) to him, hang on. The celebrants wake up with a coppery taste in their mouths. The streets are still dusty and potholed. The same twisted-limbed beggars haunt the corners. There is too little work and too little money. Independence has come, but the texture of life feels the same. That was the postindependence story of Somalia.

Mutilation of the Pan-Somali Dream

In its pursuit of Somali unification, as in its nominal quest for economic development, the civilian government failed. But in the former case, the responsibility for failure lay not in itself but in its stars: forces beyond the reach of any Somali diplomacy were completing their disintegrating work.

KENYA'S SOMALIS

Following the independence and the unification of the north and south, the principal focus of pan-Somali concern shifted to the Northern Frontier District (NFD) of Kenya and to the Ogaden. The NFD — comprising over a third of Kenya's territory but including less than ten, perhaps no more than five, percent of its population and an even more negligible proportion of its wealth — had a long history of separate administration under the umbrella of Kenya's colonial government. Over sixty percent of its 400,000-odd inhabitants were ethnic Somalis; cultural and religious ties bound a substantial percentage of the remainder to the Somali majority. Since the early part of the century, movement into and out of the region had been carefully controlled, primarily to prevent any further Somali migration southward.

By 1960, the independence of Kenya had become an issue not of whether but of when. While there was as yet no firm date, everyone saw the accelerated political pace.

Representatives of the NFD's population had stood aloof from the nationalist movements in the rest of the colony. Now, with independence close, they began to assert a distinct nationalist animus. Warmly supported from Mogadishu, a demonstrable majority demanded the right to choose association with their kin or cultural cousins in the Somali Republic and optimistically anticipated an affirmative response.

Somali optimism was reinforced when Reginald Maudling, the British secretary of state for colonial affairs, admitted an official NFD delegation to the 1962 constitutional conference and, at its conclusion, announced in a press conference that "an investigation would be undertaken in order to ascertain public opinion in the area [the NFD] regarding its future and that, for this purpose, an independent commission would be appointed as soon as possible so that its report could be available before the new constitution for Kenya was brought into operation."

Whether, in light of what followed, these gestures should be imputed to a thoroughgoing mendacity or a genuine conflict of opinion within the British government is to this day unclear. The

linchpin of British policy in Kenya was the maintenance of an atmosphere conducive to warm relations with the postindependence
government. Consequently, once British officials concluded that
self-determination for the NFD threatened future entente with
Kenya's political elite, their choice was predetermined. There is
uncertainty only over the question of when they finally decided that
self-determination and paramount British interests were incompatible.

A British decision in the 1950s to offer the NFD Somalis the option of joining their kinsmen might well have seemed a matter of
secondary concern to Kenyan nationalists, then busily engaged in
constructing effective parties, competing among themselves, and
pushing the United Kingdom toward a formal concession to majority rule within a stated and not-too-distant time. The British could,
moreover, have sweetened the pot by combining an independence
referendum in the NFD with one in the rest of the colony, thus offering the nationalists an opportunity to demonstrate the force of
independence sentiment. Even as late as the constitutional conference, when there still was no specific date for independence,
British recognition of the peculiar status of the NFD and of a consequent right to decouple from the rest of the colony might not have
irreparably damaged relations with the nationalists, particularly if
it had coincided with the announcement of a firm independence
date for the remainder of the colony. True, Jomo Kenyatta and the
other nationalist leaders were already on record as opposing any
cession of Kenyan territory. But their internal struggles, the
varieties of British leverage, their willingness to remain at the constitutional conference despite the presence of a separate NFD
delegation, and their mild response to Maudling's postconference
declaration all support the belief that it was not too late for Britain
to remove this source of future conflict.

The opportunity was lost. Months passed without the appointment of a commission. The British government deflected a steady
stream of inquiries and remonstrances from Mogadishu. In Kenya,
the march toward independence became a stampede. Its im-
minence hardened nationalist opinion about any diminution of
"their" territory. Every inch was sacred. The nationalists feared,
moreover, the consequence for their delicately poised tribal politics
of a separatist movement anywhere in the colony. If the Somalis,
then why not the coastal people, united in their fear of Kikuyu
domination?

At last, the promised commission arrived. Publicly, it had the
mandate promised by Maudling. Surreptitiously, it was instructed
that there could be no question of secession before Kenya received

independence, a restriction which appeared to be in direct conflict with the colonial secretary's announcement at the conclusion of the constitutional conference.

In their report, the commissioners found that the Somalis, who they estimated made up sixty-two percent of the NFD's population, "almost unanimously" favored secession from Kenya with the object of "ultimately" joining the Somali Republic. Their preference was shared by a majority of the smaller Muslim communities. The population of two of the area's six districts was virtually unanimous in favoring secession. In three others, there were large majorities so inclined.

The report deterred the march of events not at all. A series of unpromising communications from London began to erode the determined optimism hitherto prevailing in Mogadishu. The climax came in March, 1963, some three months after publication of the report, when the new colonial secretary, Duncan Sandys, announced that the NFD would be brought within the framework of Kenya's new constitution which emphasized the decentralization of power on a regional basis. Somali sentiment was to be accommodated by treating the predominantly Somali sections of the NFD as a distinct region.

The announcement, transmitted to Somalia by the Kenya Broadcasting Corporation, provoked angry and in some cases violent demonstrations throughout the republic. Within six days the Somali National Assembly voted 70 to 14 for a break in diplomatic relations with Britain. After consulting Satow's classic guide to diplomatic etiquette — which rumor has it had to be borrowed from the British embassy — the formalities were rapidly concluded, the ambassador packed his bags, and, on departing, complimented the Somali government for "a most civilized rupture." Along with his personal effects, he took the £1.5 million of British foreign assistance.

Nine months later, independence came to Kenya. Celebrants danced in the streets of Nairobi. But in the NFD, revolt flowered like the bush after the rains.

It was all very brave and in the end very futile. Of the suppression there is no really authoritative account. It still took a pass to get into the area from Kenya, and passes were rarely issued to people not on official business. The terrain was difficult, roads few, movement without escort dangerous. Anyway, as long as the situation promised not to get out of hand, no one other than Somalis cared very much about what was going on. The official word from Nairobi described the violence as the work of *shifta,* the Horn's generic term for raiders of every kind. Songs and poems on Radio

Mogadishu praised the "freedom fighters." The Somali government indicted the cruel repression of its kinsmen, being careful, however, to place the main onus on Britain.

Although this attribution of responsibility functioned in part as a euphemism preserving the forms of pan-African brotherhood, it also contained a large dose of truth. Having created the conditions which made revolt inevitable, the British now provided the military means for its suppression: not only the logistics, the weapons, the ammunition, the spares, and the strategy but also officers to supplement the handful of trained Kenyans. They adapted to the conditions of the Northern Frontier District techniques of counterinsurgency already tested in places like Malaya. They exploited the Somali's dependence on his animals, on the exiguous sources of water, and on his communal ties — in short, the whole fabric of his existence. Military units controlled access to the few important watering places. The authorities seized cattle and camels as collective punishment of the clans for acts attributed to any member. And they restricted the normal movement of the nomads, forcing them to bunch up near well-guarded population centers. "Rather rough, but damned effective!" was the way one knowledgeable British diplomat later summarized the campaign.

The Somali press and radio across the border blared defiance, but there was little the government could offer in terms of concrete assistance other than sanctuary and perhaps a very modest amount of ordnance. Its army was powerless: no armor, primitive logistics, little fuel, an armory of antiquated weapons, a handful of trained officers, and a few thousand lightly armed and poorly organized troops.

And so the revolt died. Not all at once, just a progressive though jagged decline of incidents to the level of a police problem. Within a year, it was clear that as long as power in Nairobi escaped fragmentation through conflict among the main Kenyan tribes, the Somalis of the NFD could never by themselves manage to detach their land from Kenya. Unification of the Somali nation would have to await accretions of strength to the Somali state, a fact lost neither on Jomo Kenyatta nor on his neighbor and generational peer, Haile Selassie. In late 1964, they signed a mutual defense agreement.

ETHIOPIA'S SOMALIS

The old empire and the new Somali Republic had difficulty preserving even the forms of pan-African amity. Achievement of a sovereign political structure in part of their cultural domain had not altered the rancid quality of the Somalis' relationship with their

Amhara neighbors. Exchanges along their entire interface had progressed from bad to worse through the 1950s as the government in Addis displayed a firm intention and increasing capacity to control all the Somalis on its side of the frontiers.

The precise location of those frontiers was one point of contention left to fester into the next decade. In the course of negotiating the 1948 protocol which governed British evacuation of the Ogaden, the parties had decided to fix a provisional boundary "without prejudice to the international frontiers between Ethiopia and former Italian Somaliland." The line was projected south from a point on the British Somaliland border at the cross section of the forty-seventh parallel and the eighth meridian, the point designated by a 1931 Anglo-Italian boundary commission as the trijunction point between Ethiopia and British and Italian Somalilands. The boundary then proceeded south at such an angle as to leave on the Ethiopian side one hundred kilometers of Ogaden territory effectively occupied and openly administered by Italy without official protest from Ethiopia or any other state for years before the outbreak of the Italo-Ethiopian war. The line actually chosen corresponded generally with Italy's interpretation of its 1908 clarifying agreement.

Before handing over the administration of Somalia to Italy in 1950, the British unilaterally altered the line by choosing a new, more-easterly trijunction point on the northern frontier, thus further enlarging the territory open to Ethiopian administration. Although the British reaffirmed the provisional and nonprejudicial character of the line, Italy expressed its strongest reservations. Not to be outdone, the Emperor laid claim to over 40,000 additional square miles of Somali-occupied territory.

When approving the trusteeship agreement for Somalia, the United Nations General Assembly had recommended that the Ethiopian and Italian governments pursue a settlement of their border dispute through direct negotiation and, if that failed, through mediation and finally, if necessary, arbitration. In each of the five succeeding years, the General Assembly urged speedy resolution of the controversy. Negotiations, after finally commencing in 1955, quickly stumbled to a halt when the Ethiopians objected categorically to the inclusion of Somalis in the Italian delegation. Eventually the Emperor relented, but it soon became evident that negotiation was not a possible route to settlement. The Ethiopian government insisted that the location of the frontier was a narrow, strictly legal issue: interpretation of the 1908 convention. It rejected the Italian claim that subsequent de facto Italian jurisdiction in the Ogaden and subsequent agreements between Italy and the

United Kingdom concerning the location of the frontier (basically the 1931 commission report) and "the needs of the local population" were equally relevant considerations.

When, in 1957, the two parties reported the failure of their negotiations to the General Assembly, the Assembly approved an Ethiopian proposal for immediate recourse to arbitration. A distinguished arbitral panel was formed the following year; it could not, however, act until the parties reached agreement on its terms of reference. And since the two parties continued to disagree hopelessly about the original meaning of the 1908 convention and about the relevance of other factors — paramount among them being the interests and preferences of the local population — their attempt to negotiate terms of reference simply completed the circle of futility. When, two years after the panel's creation, Somalia achieved independence, the dispute was still unresolved, the borders still in name "provisional."

The new republic challenged its northern as well as its southern border with Ethiopia. Just prior to independence, Somali officials in the British Protectorate had announced that they would not feel bound by the 1897 agreement between Ethiopia and Britain or the more recent confirmation thereof. The unified government of Somalia clung to that position after independence, despite threats from the Emperor to suspend free movement into traditional grazing areas. After independence, the annual migrations continued with little more than the normal level of Ethiopian molestation, molestation which lent a poignant urgency to this controversy over ownership of a seemingly valueless *tranche* of burnt bush. A staff correspondent from the London *Times,* who visited the Haud accompanied by Ethiopian officials, wrote in 1956:

> Individual tribesmen have been brutally treated (it is not possible to describe the intensely painful and humiliating torture) and Ethiopian police have attacked the tribal women. British liaison officers have been threatened by armed police, and attempts have been made to overwhelm and disarm the British tribal policemen. The most recent and serious development has been a blatant attempt to suborn the British tribes. In the case of the Habr Awal, the Ethiopian authorities tried to foist upon it some settled and partly detribalised members as Sultan and elders, a plan that strikes at the roots of the tribal organisation and loyalty. At the same time, an intertribal meeting was called without notifying the British liaison officers, and Ethiopian officials, alternating between threats and promises, tried to persuade the tribesmen to accept Ethiopian nationality . . . . [1]

The behavior described here appears to have remained fairly typical wherever Amhara troops and police have operated in culturally distinct, primarily Muslim areas, though, to be fair, one must concede the inevitably anecdotal and circumstantial character of the evidence.

The treatment of Muslims by local officials, police, and troops was in step with the Emperor's evident distaste for cultural pluralism. During a 1956 swing through the Ogaden, the Emperor had expressed dissatisfaction with the necessity of employing a Somali interpreter, and he urged his auditors to learn Amharic. In the same year, his government dispatched a UNESCO expert to visit schools in the Somali area in order to study Somali folk music with a view to "integrating" it with the music of the Amhara highlands.

The Emperor's views were not idiosyncratic. Assimilation, particularly of elites, has been a consistent tool of Ethiopian policy. Assimilation has meant mastery of one of the two elite languages — Amharic and Tigrinya (since Menelik and the shift of power to Shoa, only the former really counts) — and at least nominal induction into the Coptic church. Assimilation, understood as the promotion of Amhara cultural integrity, seems to have been an end in itself and also a valued means for preserving the political integrity and the social structure of the highland state. It had diffused the Galla threat. The Emperor clearly hoped that the Somalis too could become good Ethiopians, although he may and certainly he should have suspected that their commitment to Islam would make them far more difficult objects of an assimilationist policy than the largely pagan Gallas. But that must have seemed a minor obstacle compared to an independent Somali state on the border of Ethiopia, certain by virtue of its very existence to excite the nationalist sentiment of all Somalis and equally certain to encourage the political expression of that sentiment.

As generally anticipated, from the inception of Somali independence the border crackled with tension while violence flared across the Ogaden. Events duplicated those in the NFD. Somali clansmen harassed and were harassed by Ethiopian troops. Armed clashes proliferated. Ogaden guerrilla leaders found sanctuary and support across the border. The Somali radio roared encouragement to the "freedom fighters." Addis condemned Somali instigation of violence. Mogadishu condemned Ethiopian suppression of self-determination.

Aside from the more open character of the rhetorical antagonism between the two African capitals, the principal difference between the Ogaden and NFD conflicts was the direct involvement of the Somali Republic's armed forces in the former. In 1961 and again in 1964, Somalia and Ethiopia seemed to tremble on the edge of full-scale war. Military units met in bloody combat on the border. Naturally, in each case both sides traced the violence to an aggressive intrusion by the other. The fact that the 1961 collision occurred during an attempted coup in Addis lends credence to Ethiopian allegations of a Somali effort to exploit the confused situation in Ethiopia through probes designed to test the cohesion of the Ethiopian army. More obscure is the immediate cause of the savage exchange of blows in 1964 which included strikes inside Somali territory by the Ethiopian air force.

While there probably were distinct precipitating factors for each of these battles, it is equally probable that with a partially undemarcated border which in any case one party rejected, with troops or paramilitary forces parked on both sides of the disputed frontier engaging in periodic skirmishes, with nomads who could also be guerrillas wandering back and forth on their immemorial rounds carrying reports and sometimes the signs of Ethiopian atrocities, with an Emperor determined to consolidate his grip on this unruly territory and operating through a political apparatus which sucked revenues up to the center from the periphery and in return sent more rapacious administrators, inevitably there would be periodic outbursts of hot war. And given the disequilibrium of forces, it was not merely probable but inevitable that the Somali Republic's forces, however bravely they fought, would be thrashed. It was inevitable, that is, until the Somalis could find a donor willing to alter Ethiopian preponderance.

FRANCE'S SOMALIS

Aside from the port of Djibouti, French Somaliland or the Territory of the Afars and the Issas (TFAI)[2] has languished in an obscurity adequately justified by its size and resources.* The entire territory covers an area of some 8,500 square miles, of which ninety percent is lava-strewn desert and most of the remainder suitable only for grazing. Members of the Somali Issa clan who are numerically preponderant in the southern part of the territory around the coastal city of Djibouti, number anywhere from 50,000 to 80,000** out of a total population estimated in The 1975 *States-*

---

*As one wit put it, when the French arrived, the territory's "sole inhabitant was a jackal dying of hunger under a thorn tree."

**At least partially in order to restrict the electoral role of ethnic Somalis, thousands of the Issas are treated by the French as temporary residents. A vivid illustration of gross uncertainties about the overall size and ethnic breakdown of *man's Year Book* at 156,000. Their ethnic cousins and Muslim co-religionists, the Afars (or, as they are often called, the Danakils), cluster in the north and west where they straddle the borders with Ethiopia and Eritrea. Probably some number between 40 and 70 thousand live in the TFAI side of the frontier. In addition, there is a European population of about 10,000, perhaps 5,000 members of the French armed forces (although the figure naturally varies over time), and 8,000 Arabs, in addition to smaller numbers of the usual Mediterranean mélange — Greeks, Lebanese, etc. — that has for centuries carried on commercial ventures along the East and West African coasts.

When the French arrived in the middle of the nineteenth century, they found a series of small independent chiefdoms and sultanates which maintained trading relations with the Ethiopian interior. Beginning a little below the port of Assab, the French extended their authority south through a series of treaties, first with the local Afar potentates and then with the elders of the Somali Issa clan, until they confronted the British. Then, as noted earlier, the two powers divided their spheres with Djibouti going to France. And shortly thereafter, in 1897, a Franco-Ethiopian treaty narrowed and coincidentally confirmed the territory's western frontier.

Recent Ethiopian claims to the exercise of a historical suzerainty over the coast terminated only by French intrusion are mendacious. While it does appear that prior to the nineteenth century some of the northern Afar tribes in the area now called Eritrea conceded a nominal subjection to the rulers of Tigre, those farther south remained independent for centuries prior to French occupation of the coast and Shoan expansion from the interior. In 1895, Menelik conquered the sultan of Aussa, traditionally the most influential Afar leader, and forced him thereafter to pay tribute.

The Franco-Ethiopian entente assumed a powerfully symbiotic economic dimension in 1916 with the completion of the Djibouti-Addis rail link which established the French port as the principal outlet for Ethiopian trade. The nearby Somali port of Zeila, once a major terminus for caravans from the interior, sank into desuetude. Because of the rail link, over a third of Ethiopia's external trade still passes through Djibouti, despite the growth of Massawa and Assab. Aside from Ethiopia's transit trade, the ter-

the TFAI's population was provided inadvertently by stories appearing on consecutive pages of the *New York Times* on July 11, 1976. A story on page 4 had the Issas "numbering some 60,000 among a total population of 125,000." Another on page 5 stated that there are 70,000 Afars, and about 80,000 Issas out of a "total territorial population of 220,000."

ritory's economy relies on bunkering, the military garrison's requirements for goods and services, and a large subsidy from the French government.

Buffered against external forces physically by its interior desert and politically by its size, poverty, passivity, and perpetually amiable relations with Ethiopia, until recently the territory was unaffected by the political turbulence swirling around it. Internal forces also tended toward a seemingly endless stability. Most of the Afars maintained their politically fragmented, tradition bound pastoral existence far from the capital and the political currents of the modern world. Over half of the Somalis, on the other hand, lived in Djibouti where they filled the lower echelons of commerce and administration. Although economically deprived relative to the French and the Levantine trading community, they nevertheless enjoyed a standard of living manifestly superior to that of their fellow Somalis across the border.

Djibouti's subsidized economy was a magnet for the Somalis from the British Protectorate, some of whom worked in the port for years while remitting part of their incomes and maintaining second homes across the border. The degree to which comparative prosperity seemed a function of both army expenditure and metropolitan subsidy probably dampened Somali enthusiasm for a fundamental change in political status and thus may have helped DeGaulle's government to extract a "oui" from the territory's electorate in the 1958 referendum held throughout France's African possessions on the question of continued association with the motherland.

The referendum followed within a year the establishment of an elected legislature responsible for internal affairs. Both of the main parties in the first legislative election were led by Somalis and represented a cross-communal coalition of Somalis, Afars, and Arabs. After the election, the new assembly elected eight of its members — four Somalis (including the leader of the most successful party), two Afars, one Arab, and one European — to the new executive organ, the Council of Ministers, which was formed under the presidency of the colonial governor. Mohammed Harbi, the party leader, became vice-president.

An apparent quickening of Somali nationalist sentiment, stimulated by the pell-mell rush to independence in the protectorate, led within twelve months to a complete reshuffling of the political elements.

The chance occurrence of a referendum inspired by forces entirely exogamous to the territory's affairs gave focus to the new current of Somali nationalist feeling. Mohammed Harbi campaigned for a *"non"* vote by stressing the connection between loosened ties with France and eventual union with Somalia. His main opponent in the earlier election, Hassan Guled, led the opposition canvass, but this time he enjoyed the determined support of the French administration and the resident European population. With only 15,833 names on the electoral register (including Europeans), a vote of 8,661 was sufficient to carry the day for French Somaliland's continuation as an "Overseas Territory within the French Community." With this victory in hand, the French authorities dissolved the assembly and arranged for new elections under a new system of allocating seats. Harbi's party, operating in an environment where the economic life of most people depended on the good will of the administration and the French community, began quickly to disintegrate, a process only hastened by its defeat in the new elections by Hassan Guled's coalition party which was now showing a strong tilt toward the Afar community. After serving briefly as vice-president of the council, Guled was elected to the French Assembly and was succeeded by an Afar, although Somalis still had a slight plurality in the assembly.

It was at this juncture that the French began to demonstrate special solicitude for the comparatively more backward Afar community. Among measures designed to promote its interests was the redrawing of electoral boundaries which produced an emphatic reversal of the Somali plurality and moved a reporter for *Le Monde* to refer to "the semi-official support of the administrative authorities" for the Afar political leaders.

The administration's efforts to promote political developments conducive to an indefinite French presence were clearly consistent with the announced aims of the French government. While visiting the territory in 1959, President DeGaulle had stated flatly that France had no intention of relinquishing control over the place, to which it attached great importance. He had, of course, said pretty much the same thing about Algeria. But while *Algérie française* became just plain Algeria, French Somaliland remained unabashedly French. Reviewing a military parade in Djibouti six years after DeGaulle's visit, Pierre Messmer, then France's minister of defense, declared: "France possesses all the military potentialities to beat off any attack whatever and wherever it comes from and will stay in this country as long as she wants to." He then proceeded to Addis for talks with the Emperor, at the conclusion of which he stated that he had conveyed to the Emperor France's determination to remain in Djibouti: "The Sovereign did not object and our interview went on cordially."

President DeGaulle's visit to the territory in August, 1966, lanced the boil of accumulated Somali grievances. When their spokesmen were denied an opportunity to meet with the president, Somalis turned the popular reception planned by the administration into a hostile mass demonstration which escalated into a violent confrontation with French security forces. After suppressing the outburst, the authorities moved quickly and ruthlessly to reinforce their control. Police and troops roamed the city streets and smashed their way into houses, rounding up Somalis who could not prove their citizenship. A lifetime of residence would not suffice. Anyone who could not produce official documents was deemed an illegal alien, although up to that moment the authorities had been notoriously casual about movement and documentation. Somali Republic officials later alleged that even where documents were produced, they were sometimes confiscated by the French police.

Without benefit of formal procedure, of hearing and appeal — indeed, in many cases without benefit of any procedure other than an on-the-spot determination by arresting officers — hundreds, more likely thousands, of men, women, and children were marched to border crossing points and forcibly expelled, leaving behind family and friends, jobs, homes, and personal property. The Somali government responded by closing the border, whereupon the French authorities set up concentration camps outside Djibouti. After collecting a large catch of "illegal aliens," the French took them to a trackless part of the border and pushed them across at gun point. From there they were forced to wander on foot through a semidesert until the survivors reached cross-border villages.

The Somali government contends that within a few months of DeGaulle's abortive visit, the French expelled between 12,000 and 18,000 Somalis from the territory. While any figure is bound to be a very rough estimate, it seems generally agreed that at an absolute minimum the Somali victims of French revenge numbered in the several thousands.[3]

In addition to reducing the Somali population, the French imprisoned nationalist leaders whose status as legal residents was unimpeachable. It was in this atmosphere of violent intimidation that the French conducted the March, 1967, plebiscite in which the inhabitants of what in December, 1966, had by French ukase suddenly become the "Land of the Afars and Issas" again rejected independence. French residents, members of the French armed forces, and their families were among the eligible voters. Mogadishu screamed, "Foul!" but the Franco-Ethiopian entente and the Francophile clients of the Quai d'Orsay who then governed almost all of the nominally independent former French colonies in West Africa insulated the French government from condemnation in international or regional forums.

Democracy's End

In June, 1967, the Somali National Assembly elected a former prime minister, Abdirashid Ali Shermarke, to the presidency of the republic. Having risen again to power in part by indicting the incumbent and his allied prime minister (Shermarke's successor in that position) for insufficient militancy on the issue of Somali unity, the new president and his successful nominee for the prime ministership, Mohammed Ibrahim Egal, set busily about conciliating the main enemies of the pan-Somali dream.

They had little choice. The black African states had repeatedly aligned themselves behind Kenyatta and Selassie. The Arab states, never more than distantly sympathetic, were paralyzed now by the results of the June war. Rhetorical belligerence in Mogadishu and insurgency in the NFD and the Ogaden had produced nothing but grief for the Somalis of Kenya and Ethiopia. The Kenyan government claims that from 1963 to 1967 its security forces killed over 2,000 *shifta*. Casualty figures for the Ogaden are unknown. And given the style of Ethiopian administration and the perpetual hostility between the nomads and the Amhara-officered troops sent to keep them in line, some conflict would have occurred even without Mogadishu's encouragement. All one can say with assurance is that Somali government support had not diminished and may have encouraged Ethiopian determination to push assimilation and to assert its authority in every corner of the Ogaden.

The persistent failure of an active pan-Somali policy and the continuing economic stagnation were reinforced as catalysts of a new foreign policy by the economic stringency resulting from the Suez Canal's closure. Somalia's exports of bananas to Europe declined from 94,000 tons in 1966 to 84,000 in 1967, despite the abolition by the government of export duties on bananas, which in the past had yielded almost a million dollars annually in government revenue. The profitability of that export trade was further reduced by the increased cost of packing material and by increased wastage at sea (from fifteen to thirty-five percent) due to the longer transit time.

Shortly after securing parliamentary approval of his new government, Prime Minister Egal used the occasion of a meeting of the Organization of African Unity (OAU) to initiate discussions with both of Somalia's adversaries. Under the aegis of Zambia's president, Kenneth Kaunda, there was an initial exchange of views which the Kenyans followed quickly by a meeting in the Tanzanian city of Arusha between Egal and Kenyatta. In a formal memorandum of understanding the parties recognized the need to restore amicable relations by stopping all hostile propaganda, gradually phasing out the state of emergency in the border areas, reopening diplomatic relations, creating a committee to review periodically ways and means of furthering the development of good relations, and encouraging the growth of economic and trade ties.

On arriving back in Mogadishu, Egal was received with rather less acclaim than another peacemaker, Neville Chamberlain, had enjoyed on his return from a south German city promising "peace in our time." But despite bitter opposition from those who saw the Arusha memorandum as a sellout, Egal and the president extracted a vote of confidence from the National Assembly.

Unlike Chamberlain's Munich agreement, the Arusha memorandum was an accurate harbinger of improved relations. The two governments rapidly restored trade ties. Provocative poems and songs disappeared from the Somali radio. Kenya lifted the four-year-old state of emergency in the NFD, where calm now prevailed, and proclaimed an amnesty for all guerrillas. The demarche culminated in a state visit to Nairobi in July, 1968, by President Shermarke and Prime Minister Egal.

On the Ethiopian front, progress was less dramatic but still substantial. Initial talks followed by Mogadishu's cessation of hostile broadcasts cleared the air for an official visit by Egal to Addis two months after his appearance in Nairobi. During his visit, Egal and the Emperor agreed to establish direct telecommunication and commercial air links and to promote trade. The Emperor also agreed to lift the state of emergency in the border region. Egal undoubtedly hoped that this would lead in turn to a reduction in the number of violent encounters between Ethiopian security forces and Somali nomads. But whether because of the Emperor's determination to reduce the nomads' independence or his failure adequately to control local officials, reports of Ethiopian-inflicted casualities still flooded across the border periodically to threaten the political foundations of détente.

In their *Area Handbook for Somalia,* a team of scholars working under the auspices of the American University claim that "the

1969 elections were the most impressive in the country's history."[4] Almost 900,000 voters were able to choose among sixty-four parties, including three or four serious coalitions plus a plethora of splinter groups, many representing no more than the entourage of a single local candidate unable to secure adoption by one of the recognized parties. Led by Prime Minister Egal and President Shermarke, the Somali Youth League (SYL) emerged once again with an overwhelming preponderance of assembly seats. And as had happened following previous elections, unaffiliated parliamentarians flocked to join the majority, so that shortly after the election the SYL parliamentary group of 73 swelled to 109 out of a total of 123 seats. By the eve of the June vote to confirm the new Egal government, the largest opposition party had joined the scramble for majority favor to produce an SYL bloc of 120. Although this figure shrank following announcement of the composition of Egal's cabinet, to an outsider the election and its aftermath must have seemed an unassailable mandate for the policies of Egal and Shermarke.

In fact, however, the election was marred by credible charges of pervasive fraud and intimidation. In response to what he regarded as flagrant efforts by the prime minister and the president to employ the police force for partisan purposes, its widely respected commander, Gen. Mohammed Abshir, submitted his resignation early in the electoral campaign. During the ensuing uproar, supporters of the government accused the general of failing to follow the directives of the minister of the interior. After intensive maneuvering, a wealthy SYL power-broker, Haji Mussa Boghor, negotiated a compromise: Abshir agreed not to demand acceptance of his resignation; instead, he would take a leave of absence as police commander until after the election.

With Abshir temporarily out of the way, Shermarke and Egal shuffled senior police officials, apparently to assure the presence of pliable commanders in key election districts. The commander of the northern region, Col. Jama Mohammed Khalib, a man noted for his integrity, efficiency, and political neutrality, was recalled to administrative tasks in Mogadishu.

Authoritative sources believe that these interventions in police operations created a mood of deep bitterness in the officer cadre. Police morale could hardly have been improved by Shermarke's announcement after the election of his acceptance of Abshir's "resignation." Apparently, the president had retained that resignation letter for future use, despite the compromise. Under Abshir's dedicated leadership, the police had been a pillar of Somali democracy. Now, in their enthusiasm for electoral achievement, Egal and

Shermarke had undermined it, and tainted an election they might well have won in any event. They would soon reap the whirlwind.

The end of Somali parliamentary democracy came with dramatic suddenness. On October 15, 1969, four months after Egal's confirmation by the new assembly, President Shermarke was assassinated during a visit to a drought-stricken district in the north, the area alleged to have been the major scene of electoral shenanigans. Prime Minister Egal, then visiting the United States, hastened back to join the other SYL leaders anxious to select a new president. Late on the night of the twentieth, word leaked out that the meeting of party notables had selected Haji Mussa Boghor, paragon of the old order, as Shermarke's successor.

Before dawn, Mogadishu was in the hands of the army. Its tanks clanked up the hill in the rear of the city to surround the national police headquarters and the radio station. Although uninvolved in the organization of the coup, the police were in no mood to resist. The acting police commander, Gen. Jama Korshell, a northerner, joined the Supreme Revolutionary Council under the presidency of the coup leader, Maj. Gen. Mohammed Siad Barre, hitherto commander of the Somali armed forces.

The roundup of politicians did not stop with Egal and his supporters. Joining them as coerced guests at the president's summer residence in the nearby town of Afgoi were the two leaders of the anti-Shermarke forces in Somali politics, former President Aden Abdullah Osman and former Prime Minister Abdirazak Haji Hussein. And if any further evidence were required to document General Barre's intention of effecting revolutionary change in the old order, it was supplied when he placed General Abshir under house arrest.

Notes

1.   *The Times* (London) , October 27, 1956.

2.   For a useful overall view of French Somaliland, see Virginia Thompson and Richard Adloff, *Djibouti and the Horn of Africa* (Stanford, California: Stanford University Press, 1968) .

3.   See I. M. Lewis, "The Referendum in French Somaliland: Aftermath and Prospects in the Somali Dispute," *World Today* 23 (July 1967) :310 and "Prospects in the Horn," *Africa Report,* April 1967, p. 37; Thompson and Adloff, *op. cit.,* pp. 94-5; and Paul Mousset, "Referendum à Djibouti," *Revue des Deux Mondes,* April 15, 1967, p. 488.

4.   Irving Kaplan *et al, Area Handbook for Somalia* (Washington, D.C.: American University Foreign Area Studies, 1969) , p. 228.

Somali Under the Junta   6

National Socialism

After securing power, the junta under President Mohammed Siad Barre's leadership declared its intention to implement policies described as "scientific socialism." Since even a careful search conducted by the late Sherlock Holmes would fail to unearth either a recognizable proletariat or any economic heights to be dominated in Somalia, most of the classic Marxist and socialist ideas have little relevance to the country's actual circumstances. In practice, scientific socialism has meant efforts to mobilize all Somalis for public works activity and to mobilize students for a campaign against illiteracy. It has also meant promotion of agricultural cooperatives and increased cultivation in other forms; nationalization of most of the small commercial sector; and a far-flung program of indoctrination in the virtues of self-help, mutual cooperation, and loyalty to the nation and the regime.

The regime's apex is the Supreme Revolutionary Council (SRC), consisting of twenty-one army and police officers. It is the fountainhead of public policy. Policy is elaborated and implemented by a conventional set of ministries, each headed by a secretary of state. Younger and better-educated than their predecessors, often with English or U.S. educational backgrounds, the secretaries are the regime's technocrats. Through their bureaucracies, they conduct the day-to-day business of government.

There are, however, two activities which fall outside their domain: internal security and political indoctrination. The former is the province of the National Security Service, headed by Col. Ahmed Suleiman Abdulle (President Barre's son-in-law) and composed of carefully selected men from the police and army. Western diplomatic sources and some unofficial Horn-watchers believe (with varying degrees of confidence) that Soviet KGB officers helped to design the service and now function as advisers. Indoctrination has been carried out by politically reliable cadres operating in provincial and district centers and responsible directly to the SRC. According to reports from Mogadishu, President Barre has finally decided to launch a political party which will assume responsibility for the indoctrination function.

Another agent of SRC policy operating outside the civil bureaucracy is a kind of youth militia, the Gul-wa-dayasha ("Victory Pioneers"). Its main tasks seem to be mobilizing the population for the compulsory essays in self-help and monitoring the activities of foreigners, particularly their contacts with Somalis. A recent visitor to Mogadishu told me that outside his hotel he was under constant surveillance. On one occasion, having sought directions from a Somali, he turned around after taking a few steps and saw a Victory Pioneer in his distinctive green uniform interrogating the informant. Another fairly recent visitor, an Englishman who had once served in Somalia, tells of striking up a conversation with a storekeeper when the man suddenly stiffened, mumbled something about not having an item which neither had mentioned, and then hurried into the rear of the shop. The Englishman turned around to find a Victory Pioneer lounging near the door.

A marked reluctance to issue entry visas to Westerners, particularly Americans, and restraints on their mobility within Somalia function together with the close surveillance of social contacts and the tame press to hamper appraisal of the regime's achievements. It appears, however, that President Barre's government has generated an impressive momentum toward amelioration of the harsher edges of the country's poverty. In part, it is a matter of atmosphere. The good-natured, aimless languor is gone. One senses a bustling purposefulness, an unwonted hustling toward tangible goals.

There are also concrete achievements, particularly in the capital. Under the self-help program, the Somali people contribute as much as seven hours a week of their "leisure" time to government-designed projects. The results are particularly prominent in Mogadishu where one sees a new hotel, a new office complex for the Foreign Ministry, new roads and schools, housing estates, and clean streets. The government has expanded the acreage under cultivation; its goal is self-sufficiency in basic food items within three years. The emphasis on agriculture notable in the new five-year plan is not restricted to food products. Cotton, already grown on a commercial scale, is scheduled for major expansion in production.

In the fields of education and public health, progress is more striking. During 1970-71 alone, the primary school population in-

creased by one hundred percent. There has also been expansion at
the secondary and university levels. Of at least equal significance is
the war on adult illiteracy. The government mobilized students for
an initial national literacy campaign conducted for the benefit of
the settled thirty to thirty-five percent of the population. Now it
proposes to reach beyond the towns and villages to the nomadic majority. On the public health front, the incidence of malaria, tuber-
culosis, and other endemic diseases has been sharply reduced. It was
these direct contributions to the quality of Everyman's life, as well
as the widely prevailing self-help projects, which led Julius Nyerere
to remark during the 1974 meeting in Mogadishu of the OAU heads
of state: "The Somalis are practicing what we in Tanzania preach."

To what extent have these gains been paid for through a reduction in the ordinary Somali's sense of personal freedom? The short
answer is: We don't know. Such evidence as we have is largely anecdotal, impressionistic, and conflicting. Some Western observers
find the atmosphere coercive; others see enthusiasm, pride, and active support for the junta among the generality of urban Somalis.
Those who sense a high degree of coercion may or may not be pro-
jecting onto Somalis their own thoroughly accurate perception of
close surveillance with its attendant psychological discomforts.

The circumstantial evidence is extremely ambiguous. On the
one hand, acts such as the 1972 public execution of two SRC members (accused of plotting against President Barre) and the 1975 execution of ten conservative religious figures (who had indicted, as
a violation of the Koran, the government's decision to guarantee
equal rights for women) imply a feverish insecurity which in turn
suggests subterranean currents of opposition to the junta. This
assumes, of course, that where there is insecurity there is usually
something to be insecure about. On the other hand, President
Barre's 1973 decision to release most of the *ancien régime*'s political
notables from their enforced residence in what they wryly labeled
the "Afgoi Hilton" and his subsequent appointment of several of
their number to responsible administrative and diplomatic positions may reflect a solidly based confidence in widespread public
support. But since insecurity can simply be paranoid and confidence either delusive or a function of ruthless authoritarian control, one hesitates to make very much of this circumstantial
evidence.

There does appear to have been at least one instance of spontaneous resistance to government policy. In October, 1973, residents
of the northern town of Burao and of the surrounding area rioted in
response to demands that they undertake a self-help exercise in
street cleaning and that they pay taxes. In practice, the civilian

government had collected direct taxes only from civil servants. An early postindependence effort to collect the land tax encountered ardent resistance throughout the country and was quietly interred. In this case, the army intervened and, in suppressing the outburst, reportedly killed eight people. Many of the rioters were nomads only temporarily encamped in and around Burao. A large number of them are said to have responded to the crackdown by fleeing across the Ethiopian border. That is the only known demonstration of popular hostility. And since it occurred in a region whose population has been consistently unenthusiastic about Mogadishu-based governments, it is not persuasive evidence of large-scale dissatisfaction with the SRC.

An effort to extend the secular revolution to the mass of fiercely independent traditionalists out in the bush would almost surely have encountered bloody resistance. Perhaps this government would nevertheless have tried had fate not delivered the nomads into its hands.

By early 1975, it was apparent that the drought which had decimated the Sahel tribes and emptied villages in the Ethiopian heartland was well on its way to destroying the basis for life on the sere plains of the Ogaden and the adjoining Somali territory. Of the Somali Democratic Republic's approximately three million inhabitants, some 800,000 had lost the larger proportion — in many cases all — of their herds. Deaths from starvation were escalating geometrically.

In vivid contrast to Haile Selassie's precedent, the Somali government went public, pleading for international disaster relief. Simultaneously, it deployed its full resources, including the armed forces and the students spread around the country as part of the literacy and consciousness-raising campaign, to rescue and to begin the rehabilitation of the ravaged clans. Within a few months, a quarter of a million of the most desperate cases had been drawn into refugee camps run exclusively by Somali students and officials. The inmates were housed, fed, and incorporated into the literacy program.

The drought's impact had been intensified by the progressive overgrazing of the plains. It had for years been apparent that the land could not support indefinitely a growing animal and human population, much less allow a margin for development. The herds had been the basis of nomadic life. Now they were decimated beyond hope of renewal without massive external assistance. And full-scale renewal, if it did occur, would in turn aggravate the deterioration of the overgrazed land.

What opportunity offered, President Barre and his colleagues quickly took. With generous Soviet support, they transported roughly 100,000 nomads into hastily prepared agricultural settlements in the relatively fertile southern region of the country. A much smaller number, reportedly about 20,000, were settled along the coast to take up new lives as fishermen. The remainder were to have their herds restocked so that they could return to the traditional nomadic life.

Whether the transplants will hold and whether the restocked herds will survive are open questions. Indeed, the larger effort to transform Somali life, of which the resettlements are only a part, remains terribly problematic. The regime's accomplishments to date seem a function of unusually liberal Soviet support plus a degree of indigenous vision and energy with few obvious parallels in sub-Sahara Africa. But the country's economic margin remains perilously thin. And the threat of war dissipates both its slender resources and the attention of its small elite.

Defense and Foreign Policy

THE MAKING OF AN ARMY

Somalia's first benefactor in the military field was the United Arab Republic (UAR). Immediately after their independence, the Somalis were supplied with a small quantity of obsolete items from UAR inventories. The paucity and particularly the poor quality of the donated material encouraged the new state to look elsewhere for assistance.

In 1961, it received and promptly rejected a modest offer from the Czechs. An initial canvass of the NATO states produced discouraging results. The United States flatly refused Somali overtures. The United Kingdom and Italy at first seemed equally uninterested in becoming donors of military aid. In 1962, however, they reversed their positions and offered a joint program worth $8.4 million. The Somali government quickly accepted. But toward the end of the year, when the NFD crisis was sweeping United Kingdom-Somali relations toward the breakpoint, the NATO allies proposed a revised and somewhat expanded program. Under it, the United States, Italy, and West Germany would provide roughly $10 million worth of equipment and training for a force of 5,000 to 6,000 soldiers with a pronounced orientation toward civic action and internal security. In return, the Somali government would undertake not to accept military assistance from any other source.

The offer remained pending for almost a year until it was rejected coincident with the government's announcement that it had accepted a Soviet-authored alternative valued at about $32 million.

Although the specific terms of the Soviet-Somali military aid agreement were not published, its principal dimensions were generally understood to be as follows. The Soviets would train and equip with modern weapons a 10,000-man armed force, including a small air wing using jet planes. Most of the program cost would be treated as a grant with the remainder to be repaid over a twenty-year period.

News of the arms agreement was received in Addis with unconcealed anger. Despite Soviet assurances regarding the projected size of the Somali army, the Emperor accused the Russians of generating an arms race on the Horn and of preparing to underwrite a 20,000-man army capable of initiating offensive operations. Both Somali and Russian officials denied the Ethiopian allegations and reaffirmed the purely defensive character of the proposed program.

By the 1969 coup, the Somali armed forces had just about completed the build-up projected at the time of the original military aid agreement. But following the accession of President Barre, the Soviet military aid program burst through its originally programmed dimensions. By 1974, the Somali armed forces had reached the 20,000 figure angrily predicted a decade earlier by Haile Selassie, where it has more or less stabilized. The quality of its weapons also was markedly enhanced, particularly in armor and aircraft. The current inventory includes about fifty MIG fighters (among them twenty-four supersonic MIG-21s) and several Ilyushin bombers — on paper close to the strongest air-strike capacity in black Africa. How many planes are actually serviceable at any given moment is, however, uncertain, since there still are glaring maintenance deficiencies, the bugbear of all armies in technologically underdeveloped countries. Maintenance deficiencies also hurt the armored units, recently beefed up with T-54 tanks that are among the most modern in Soviet inventories.

By contrast, in 1975 the Ethiopians had only 37 combat planes, and, with the exception of 9 F-5As, they were obsolete as contestants for air superiority against the Somali MIGs. But in 1976 the Dergue has acquired or is in the process of acquiring at least 20 F5-Es, a sophisticated fighter-bomber which compares favorably with anything the Somalis can deploy. Again on paper, there was an even more dramatic difference in armor. The authoritative survey of the International Institute for Strategic Studies (IISS) [1] lists 250 medium tanks and approximately 300 armored personnel carriers in Somali inventories compared to 12 medium and 50 light tanks for the Ethiopians plus just over 100 armored personnel carriers and armored cars. However, it is likely that, by committing yet another slice of the country's financial reserves, the Dergue will narrow this gap as well. Moreover, with respect both to Somali aircraft and armor, the IISS estimates are followed by the caveat, "spares are short and not all equipment is serviceable."

The rapid build-up of Somali military capabilities required a sharp escalation in the number of Soviet advisers. From a 1969 base of well under 1,000, the total figure for military and civilian advisers has been estimated to exceed 2,000 — by how much Western sources seem unsure — although most observers disparage the more-extreme claims which edge up toward 10,000.[2]

COMPETITORS FOR INFLUENCE

While unrivaled in the military aid field, the Soviet Union is just one among several important donors of economic assistance. In 1966, the United States, acting under a congressional directive, terminated the remnants of its once substantial aid program because Somali-registered ships had carried freight to Hanoi. But Italy continued to provide significant support. And, as an associate member of the European Economic Community, Somalia has received substantial aid from the European Development Fund, which at present is financing expansion of the national university and, jointly with the World Bank, construction of a deep-water port for Mogadishu.

The Chinese have been around virtually since independence, managing through a low profile and a steady policy of political neutrality to cultivate the same engaging image they enjoy in Addis. Unlike Soviet projects which have, on occasion, antagonized the Somalis with cost overruns or other deficiencies, Chinese efforts seem well conceived and effectively implemented. By far the most ambitious Chinese project, a 1,045-kilometer road running parallel to the Ethiopian border from the old Italian outpost of Beledwein in the south (already connected to Mogadishu by an all-weather road) to Burao, is reported to be proceeding on schedule. Its projected cost of approximately $60 million makes it the most substantial Chinese venture in Africa after the Tanzam railway.

Somalia's recent accession to the Arab League has enhanced its prospects for attracting petrodollar aid. The United Arab Emirates, Libya, and Iraq have all made allegedly significant, albeit still rather indeterminate, commitments; actual disbursements have apparently lagged a good deal behind. The Saudi Arabian government flatly conditioned an aid offer of $75 million on the progressive contraction of Russian activities in Somalia. When the Somalis refused to satisfy the stipulated condition, the offer was withdrawn.

THE REGIME'S FOREIGN POLICY

Growing military strength, the appearance of impressive domestic achievements, and strengthened ties to a renascent Arab world have, in proportions unknown, catapulted the Somalis from their earlier OAU role as a kind of pitiable but irritating problem child to a member state of generally recognized importance and prestige. When, in 1973, Tanzania and Idi Amin's mercenary regime in Uganda teetered on the brink of full-scale war, it was President Barre who acted to mediate their differences. In 1975, Mogadishu was the setting for the annual gathering of the OAU heads of state; and, following precedent, they elected their colleague from the host country to serve as president of the organization for the succeeding year. Of greater significance than President Barre's essentially automatic selection was the good race run by Somali Foreign Minister Omar Arteh Ghalib, with the support of the Arab members and many of the predominantly Muslim black African states, for the vacant OAU post of secretary-general.

For Somalia, the rapid accretion of military and diplomatic clout has coincided with gathering tension along the Ethiopian border. The fresh gust of hostility is partially attributable to those increasingly ubiquitous sources of discord, oil and gas.

For almost two decades, corporate exploration teams have probed different parts of the Horn with high hopes and no success. Geological promise has remained tantalizingly unfulfilled. Most exploration activity has been strung along the Ogaden border; there has also been activity in the Northern Frontier District of Kenya. Following a succession of dry wells east of the provisional Ogaden border, exploration activity has ground to a virtual halt in Somalia. On the Ethiopian side of the border, Tenneco, a U.S. company, began drilling in February, 1972. Just over a year later, gas began pouring into a drill hole at the 11,000-foot mark. According to one unofficial report, the rate of flow extrapolated to thirty-five million cubic feet per day. A subsequent well in the area turned out dry. Tenneco officials claim that they are still evaluating the overall results.

The actual find, at a spot only thirty miles from the Somali border, threatened to tear off what remained of the scab on relations between the two neighbors. The spirit of détente, conjured into existence by Egal and Shermarke, had begun to wither from the moment Tenneco workers first arrived in the area with a guard of thirty-five Ethiopian troops, which grew quickly to over one hundred. Some observers believe that Ethiopia was concerned not only about the security of drilling operations but also about the flow of cattle across the open border to Somalia's Indian Ocean ports, a movement which hampered Ethiopian efforts to create a meat-processing industry. When Somalia countered the gradual build-up of Ethiopian forces along the border with troop concentrations of its own, the tension level between the two states rose proportionately.

An attempt in late December, 1973, and in the succeeding January to lower the diplomatic temperature through face-to-face discussions culminated in a vitriolic shouting match between negotiators. Shortly after the Ethiopian delegates had stormed back to Addis from Mogadishu, convoys of additional Ethiopian troops began to roll east to beef up the border forces.

Though braced for war, neither side seemed eager to initiate it. They came closest to open conflict the following year when the Somalis threw a contingent of about one hundred men across the border in the direction of the drilling operation. The Third Division commander responded by dispatching a larger force to the rear of the Somalis and cutting off their access to water. After several tense days, during which the Somalis made no effort to force supplies through the Ethiopian blockade, the probe was withdrawn without further incident.

As the veneer of détente peeled away to expose the old animosities, the Emperor, with the active encouragement of his officer corps, hustled about in search of more and more modern arms. The U.S. program, having settled down to a steady $11 million a year, provided spares, ammunition, training, and a certain amount of weapon replacement. On an official visit to the United States in 1973, the Emperor pressed his case for additional grant aid to allow modernization of his inventories. He returned with his fur well stroked and his hand empty. While Ethiopia, like any old friend, would always be welcome in the Pentagon's cash-and-carry department, President Nixon is reported to have said that the subbasement soup kitchen could not increase its annual dispensation. Access to the bargain basement with its concessional credit terms was left, at best, uncertain. Had the Emperor known of the already firm decision to reduce operations at Kagnew Station, he would have more readily understood the slippage in his once highly leveraged position. But it was only after he had returned to Addis that the news was conveyed to him through the American embassy.

An urgent appeal to Ethiopia's other staunch ally, Israel — which for more than a decade had cooperated with the U.S. Mili-

tary Assistance Advisory Group (MAAG) in training the Emperor's
army for, among other things, the dubious struggle in Eritrea —
evoked an equally unsatisfactory response, though for different
reasons: the Israelis simply had nothing they were able to spare.
Nor, it is reported, were they receptive to the Emperor's proposal
that they activate their influence network in the United States on
behalf of Ethiopian arms requests, a response which probably convinced the Emperor that his Israeli connection had lost its utility.
When, on Yom Kippur, 1973, the Arab armies sliced into Sinai,
Haile Selassie finally — and by all accounts reluctantly — clambered
onto the Afro-Arab bandwagon and severed diplomatic relations
with Israel.

According to one Western diplomatic source, having been rejected by his old consorts, the Emperor turned at last to a long-
frustrated suitor only to be informed by the object of his sudden affection that, as far as the Horn was concerned, the Russian bear was
already engaged. Disappointed but undeterred by his various and
unexpected rebuffs, the Emperor and his generals continued to
press the United States for additional assistance.

Within both the U.S. embassy and MAAG, opinion was sharply
split. The ambassador and his senior political advisers championed
the Ethiopian cause in the name of strategic imperatives. Several
younger foreign service officers opposed stepped-up aid. They were
impressed neither by the "Somali threat" nor by the case for
Ethiopia's continued strategic value. On the Somali issue, they
found support among U.S. military men, a number of whom insisted that, despite their new equipment, the Somalis still enjoyed
strategic inferiority. According to one experienced officer:

> They could race across the border and seize a strip of the
> Ogaden. Maybe they could surround and chop up the one divi-
> sion opposite them, although that's doubtful. The Ethiopians
> would almost surely play it smart, drop back to Harar where
> they have supplies and prepared positions, and wait for rein-
> forcements. The Somalis simply don't have the logistics to get
> very far into Ethiopia. They wouldn't get anywhere near the
> heartland. And I'll wager that once the Ethiopians concentrate
> their forces in the south, they'll push the Somalis all the way
> back across the border and maybe then some. In fact, once the
> Ethiopians get going, they might not stop until they get to the
> sea.

It is hard to tell the degree to which such sanguine assessments
are influenced by the assumption common among U.S. advisers
that the Ethiopians are superior fighters. History may seem to con-

firm their relative martial prowess, unless one recalls the overwhelming advantages enjoyed by Menelik II and Haile Selassie by
virtue of Ethiopia's access to modern arms and the society's comparatively well-knit and hierarchical organization. Among English
and Italian officers who fought alongside the Somalis during World
War II, one has no difficulty in soliciting testimonials to the valor of
their Somali colleagues.

The proportions of the Somali threat are obscured by varying
assessments not only of their military capabilities but also of their
intentions. In Mogadishu, the Somali government continues to em-
phasize its peaceful intentions and to detect an aggressive impulse
not in itself but rather in its Abyssinian neighbor. It does not
hesitate to recall Haile Selassie's postwar insistence on the natural
and historical unity of the highlands and the Benadir coast.

In light of Ethiopia's failure to press its military supremacy during the 1960s, current Somali expressions of concern may seem
something short of ingenuous. On the other hand, they reflect a
real historical experience which may have left a residue of genuine
suspicion. Moreover, within any country, as in the world at large,
militancy ebbs and flows in an often unpredictable cycle. A satisfied
Ethiopia in the 1960s, ruled by an aging emperor cultivating the
image of a benign statesman and perhaps less eager for victories
than fearful of coups, does not guarantee a peaceful Ethiopia in the
1970s and beyond, when its leaders will be younger and the global
climate perhaps more tolerant of force. And suppose the bulk of the
Horn's oil turns out to be on the Somali side of the border? Who
knows what temptations lurk over today's horizon? Perhaps President Barre and his colleagues are actually impervious to these ner-
vous speculations. Perhaps not. The evidence is inconclusive.

Notes

1.   *The Military Balance, 1975-1976* (London: The International Institute for
     Strategic Studies, 1975), p. 43.

2.   See for example, "Somalis: How Much Soviet Influence?" *Africa Confiden-
     tial,* July 6, 1973, p. 3 and *Africa Research Bulletin* (Political, Social, and
     Cultural Series), July 1974, p. 3316.

Part Three

A Policy Perspective

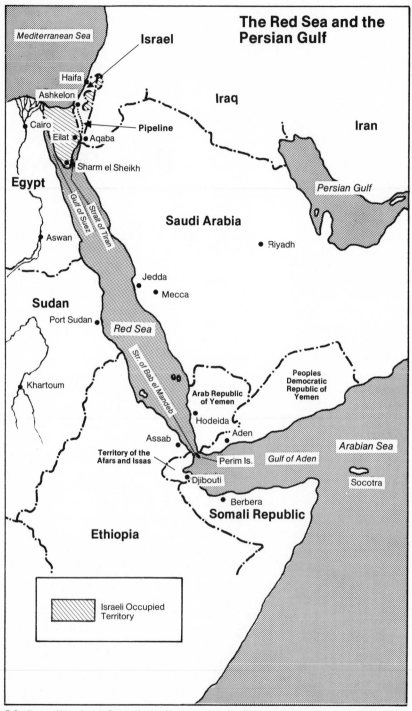

The Red Sea and the Persian Gulf

Mediterranean Sea

Israel

Haifa

Ashkelon

Cairo

Eilat • • Aqaba

Pipeline

Sharm el Sheikh

Iraq

Iran

Persian Gulf

Egypt

Gulf of Suez

Strait of Tiran

Aswan •

Saudi Arabia

• Riyadh

Jedda •

• Mecca

Sudan

Port Sudan •

Red Sea

Str. of Bab el Mandeb

Khartoum •

Peoples Democratic Republic of Yemen

Arab Republic of Yemen

Hodeida

Aden

Assab •

Territory of the Afars and Issas

Perim Is.

Gulf of Aden

Arabian Sea

Djibouti •

Socotra

Berbera •

Somali Republic

Ethiopia

Israeli Occupied Territory

The Geopolitical Context: The Indian Ocean 7

The Indian Ocean is not a Red sea. The Russians are there but with far more dubious strategic consequence than is frequently averred.

Soviet Interests

One body of expert opinion finds the main initial motive for the Soviet naval build-up, beginning in the mid-sixties, in a desire to lay the foundation for an active defense against the U.S. ballistic-missile-bearing submarines that might someday patrol the Indian Ocean.[1] For submarine-launched ballistic missiles (SLBMs) like Polaris A-3 and Poseidon,* with a range of roughly 3,000 nautical miles, the northwest quadrant of the Indian Ocean (the so-called Arabian Sea) offers coverage of potential targets in European Russia roughly equivalent to that achieved by missile-firing submarines deployed in the Mediterranean and the western approaches to the Eurasian land mass. Those missiles, together with the VLF (very low frequency) communications stations operated by the United States at the two extremities of the ocean in western Australia and Ethiopia's coastal province of Eritrea and what appeared to be a third one programmed for Diego Garcia, made Indian Ocean patrols possible.

Other factors made them conceivably attractive. They would, for example, have widened the azimuth of potential attack on the Soviet Union, thus further complicating the problematical task of constructing a reasonably effective antiballistic missile (ABM) system. In actual fact, however, Indian Ocean patrols were not then and are not today a cost-effective means for achieving that or any

---

*By the mid 1960s, these SLBMs were already in U.S. inventories.

other military objective. The northwest quadrant is simply too far away from the nearest U.S. submarine base in Guam.

Crew endurance, re-enlistment rates, and certain other factors set definite limits to the duration of a voyage. Hence, the comparatively longer time required for transit to and from the patrol area correspondingly reduces the length of time the submarine can remain on station. It thus follows that the farther the patrol area is from the nearest base, the greater the number of submarines required to assure that one is always in position to launch its missiles.

Indian Ocean patrols would be practical only if the United States could establish a submarine base with a proximity roughly comparable to Rota for Mediterranean patrols and Holy Loch for patrols off the northwestern rim of the Soviet Union. Theoretically, the only essential feature of a base is the "tender," an enormous ship — virtually a floating dry dock — staffed by the highly skilled technicians required to service a missile-launching submarine. But peacetime realities require the presence of housing as well as recreational and other facilities for dependents. Although offering the predictably benign political climate required to justify a large investment in fixed installations, a barren, claustrophobic pimple of land like Diego Garcia cannot, therefore, constitute a plausible missile-launching submarine base site. Some of the larger, more physically charming places in and around the Indian Ocean are governed by elites who deem neutrality or even a pro-Soviet tilt in East-West competition more consistent with their interests. Others are politically volatile. Still others, most notably South Africa, are pariahs to much of the world, including influential U.S. constituencies.

The evident high costs of an Indian Ocean patrol and the difficulties that would clearly attend any effort to reduce them have influenced some observers to deride the idea that the prospect of such patrols could have attracted Soviet concern. Implicit in the quiet ferocity of this recondite controversy is a larger debate over the meaning of the Soviet Union's efforts to establish a presence in the area. Those who prefer to construe the Soviet presence as a serious and immediate threat to Western interests are in general inclined to belittle the invocation of Soviet concern over SLBMs. The fantasts among these skeptics — some of whom are, as well, advocates of military collaboration with South Africa — prefer to envision a burgeoning threat to the sea lanes. Less whimsical analysts envision a Soviet plan to use naval power to erode Western influence through the classic means of encouraging friendly regimes and intimidating or facilitating the replacement of those deemed hostile.

Curiously enough, treating Soviet concern for potential U.S. SLBM patrols as an important explanation of the Soviet presence is quite compatible with the most jaundiced conception of Russian motives. Efforts to acquire the capacity to threaten our sea-based deterrent at some time in the future are not necessarily less ominous than the other theories of Soviet motivation enumerated above. In a certain tactical sense, antisubmarine warfare, is, of course, defensive. But in a strategic context, it may or may not be, depending upon the larger design of which it forms a part. Perhaps that is the problem, the fact that it *could be* defensive in intent. As a rhetorical weapon in our domestic debate over national security policy, the prospect of an attack on the West's sea lanes is flawed with none of those softening ambiguities. Hence the charm it exerts on such self-instructed authorities in the realm of Soviet military policy as Professor Moynihan.

Despite efforts to discount it, the antisubmarine hypothesis retains a plausible role in any comprehensive explanation of Soviet interests. Just as the shape of U.S. defense expenditures has sometimes been influenced decisively by worst-case projections of Soviet capabilities, the Soviets may have responded in this case to the technical feasibility of Indian Ocean patrols. They may not, after all, fully appreciate the way in which we tote up costs. Moreover, even if their analysts appreciated our probable assessments of cost effectiveness, the Russians could be laying the foundation for an unpredictable future.

It takes time to establish the political relations, the physical infrastructure, and the experience to operate effectively in a new environment. In the meantime, détente could wither and with it the restraints on ABM deployment established by the first Strategic Arms Limitation Talks (SALT I). There could, as well, be a major breakthrough in antisubmarine warfare which might provide additional incentives for the expansion of SLBM patrol areas. And for a variety of reasons, including the apparently relentless growth in economic ties between South Africa and the West, the United States might gradually discount the political costs of a submarine base in South Africa. In other words, the present inefficiency of Indian Ocean patrols would not make it irrational for the Russian Navy to develop an antisubmarine capability in that area.

Whether or not it influenced the initial decision to deploy east of Suez, development of an antisubmarine capability now appears to be a significant part of the Russian mission there. During the worldwide naval exercise called OKEAN, conducted by the Russians in 1975, this seems to have been the only function assigned to their Indian Ocean squadron.

Whatever the initial motive for the comparatively modest presence the Russians have established in the Indian Ocean,* that presence has endowed them with the means to pursue a second interest: naval diplomacy.[2] Lacking foreign bases and a blue-water fleet and doctrinally committed to the use of naval power either in defense of the Russian coastline or in direct support of ground forces operating on the Eurasian land mass, throughout the fifties and the early sixties the Russians had left the field open to the navies of their Western antagonists. But after careful preparation, moving from scattered, unprotected anchorages to well-endowed Arab bases, they joined the game through operations in the eastern Mediterranean in support of Arab friends. Following Colonel Qaddafi's coup in Libya, they were observed off the coast of that country, possibly, some analysts argue, to discourage a Western intervention in support of the deposed king. And nearer the end of the decade, by anchoring in Egyptian harbors during the war of attrition with Israel, they may have inhibited Israel's exploitation of its dominant military position.

Operations in the Mediterranean were soon extended to the Indian Ocean and the Atlantic littoral of Africa. When the government of Ghana seized two Russian fishing vessels and imprisoned their crews for alleged involvement in a rumored coup, Russian warships eventually took a leisurely cruise along the Ghanian coast in apparent support of conventional diplomatic protests. Whether they actually influenced the ultimate release of the crews is unclear.

The conflict over Bangladesh demonstrated Soviet determination to play in higher-stake games. Immediately following U.S. dispatch of carrier task force seventy-four toward the Bay of Bengal for the evident purpose of restraining the Indian government, the Russians responded with a dramatic increase in their own Indian Ocean force levels.

Clearly, the Western monopoly on naval diplomacy in the Indian Ocean has been broken. The question of whether that is a matter of much strategic consequence will shortly be examined.

Like the United States, the Soviet Union has interests in the Indian Ocean largely unrelated to superpower competition. The Russians depend far more heavily on the sea as a source of protein than do most Western states. Although less fertile than the Atlantic and the Pacific, the Indian Ocean is still an important operating area for Soviet trawlers, providing within recent years a fifth or more of

---

* For the past several years, this presence has generally been smaller than the flotilla maintained by France alone.

their catch. Once upon a time, fishing was a peaceful occupation. It rarely required the ministrations of friendly gunboats. But today, in the face of burgeoning unilateral extensions of coastal-state claims to living resources, the occasions requiring naval escorts for fishing fleets have grown exponentially. And they are likely to expand at a yet more dramatic pace if a general agreement on littoral-state jurisdiction is not achieved in the context of the Law of the Sea negotiations. Such an agreement, moreover, may only slow the pace of gathering conflict; it will probably leave many issues (such as the period of phase-out for traditional users and the size of an optimal catch) for subsequent bilateral negotiations. The consensus supporting a contemporary agreement may, moreover, erode as national populations press ever more exigently against finite resources.

No one proposes that protection of its fishing interests is a major Soviet concern. Some analysts, noting the absence of any Soviet naval presence off the coasts of Latin America, where the fishing grounds are richer and the littoral states more belligerent about extending their jurisdiction, argue that it figures not at all among Soviet interests.

While they may be right, the cited evidence is by no means compelling. The absence of securely friendly port facilities beyond Cuba, U.S. sensitivity to Soviet naval activities in the Western Hemisphere, and the danger of actually being forced to confront Latin navies (that have, after all, not been deterred even by the United States from bold assertions of exclusive fishing rights) all weigh heavily against the advantages of naval patrols in support of Soviet fishermen. Incentives in the Indian Ocean are radically different.

There is, in addition, the ocean's importance as a link in the sea route to Russia's Pacific coast and to important friendly governments, particularly in India and Vietnam. Between forty-five and fifty percent of Russian military and economic assistance now goes to Indian Ocean littoral states. For the movement of heavy equipment or oil either to such friends or to its own Asian territory, the sea route has no serious competition. To be sure, there is no present threat to that route. Nevertheless, if one conjures the long-term, worst-case scenarios so dear to the hearts of conventional strategists (in this instance, the growth of Chinese sea power), one can then visualize the argument for a protective presence probably advanced by Soviet admirals in budgetary competition with traditionally more favored branches of the Russian armed forces.

Beyond the Soviet leadership's interest in securing the country's shipping lanes looms the relentless competition with China for influence in the Afro-Asian world. The Chinese have the congenital advantage of being a colored race and the acquired advantage of a development model more engaging to idealists and, particularly in Africa, more plausibly relevant to the human condition. Moreover, having neither a blue-water fleet nor global military ambitions to service, the Chinese have no incentive to demand base rights as a condition for the extension of aid.

The Russians can attempt to overcome these advantages with potentially more bountiful aid, more advanced technology, and, thanks to their fleet, readily available muscle. Regimes can find balm in the prospect of a friendly cruiser appearing off the coast when coups are being hatched or a hostile neighbor is rattling its sabers. The Chinese can train Rhodesian guerrillas based in Mozambique. But, unlike the Soviets, they cannot offer an on-the-spot deterrent to Rhodesian or South African intervention.

Soviet Strategic Superiority?

In the Indian Ocean area, the Russian Navy suffers a double disadvantage vis-à-vis the West: overall, it has a greater need for, yet less-assured access to, littoral support facilities.

Any one of the carrier task forces the United States can deploy on extended patrol in the Indian Ocean represents air power capable of devastating any flotilla the Soviets can practicably deploy east of Suez in the near future without shore-based air support. The Soviets have only three carriers afloat. They are configured for helicopters and, perhaps, very-short-takeoff-and-landing planes with limited range and dubious ability to offset the offensive thrust of U.S. carrier-based aircraft. Moreover, until a far larger number of carriers enter service, the Soviet Navy may be reluctant to deploy any carriers so far from the present focus of naval concern—the Mediterranean and the Atlantic approaches to European Russia.

Shore facilities also have a special urgency for the Russians because of their inferior amphibious support capability. Unlike the United States, they have only an extremely limited and thoroughly makeshift capacity for under-way replenishment, plus a smaller overall service force. Furthermore, the twenty-five-percent-greater average size of U.S. ships in the destroyer-escort category probably translates into better habitability and larger on-board supplies with consequent gains in endurance. The Russians' profound dependence on surface-to-air and ship-to-ship missiles both for offensive and defensive operations, coupled with the absence of any on-board reload capacity for their anti-ship missiles (unlike comparable U.S. weapon systems), generates additional need for secure shore facilities where, among other things, missiles can be tested and stored.*

THE SOMALI CONNECTION

Soviet facilities in the Somali Democratic Republic are not essential for bunkering and minor repairs, at least in times of low tension. For those limited purposes, the Russians can use other ports such as Aden in South Yemen (PDRY), Hodeida in North Yemen, Umm Qasyr in Iraq, and, far to the south, Port Louis in Mauritius and Beira and Lourenço Marques in Mozambique. They can, moreover, use protected anchorages off the South Yemeni island of Socotra and the Maldive Islands for rendezvous and resupply. But only in Somalia will they shortly have airfields capable of handling the largest planes in their inventory;** communications facilities (which, if U.S. experience is any guide, are not yet fully replicable by satellites); a secure place for missile storage, testing, and loading; and barracks where crews can be rested or held in reserve.

All of the ingredients of a significant base are present with the possible exception of assured access under all conditions. Conceivably, there is no explicit base-rights agreement. Agreement or no, the size of the Soviet investment certainly evidences a considerable degree of confidence in a continuing welcome from the Somali government. That confidence springs from something more secure than a simple agreement or an apparent ideological congruence with the incumbent regime. It springs from Somalia's severe dependence on the Soviet Union for the supply, training, and logistical support of its armed forces.

WESTERN BASES

If Western facilities in the Indian Ocean are lumped together, which for certain contingencies is realistic, they constitute a far more substantial infrastructure than the Russians have been able to assemble. The American base on Diego Garcia boasts a sophisticated communications facility and an 8,000-foot runway supporting reconnaissance patrols over most of the ocean. The runway will be extended to the 12,000 feet required for KC-135 aerial tankers, and the lagoon will be equipped for the anchorage, bunkering, and supply of a carrier and its support ships.

---

*Anti-ship and anti-aircraft missiles lack the reliability required for combat effectiveness if they are not routinely disassembled and tested.

**One airfield, configured primarily for fighters, is already operational.

Inside the Persian Gulf at Bahrain, the United States maintains its so-called Mideast Force, consisting of a converted amphibious ship serving as flagship and two destroyers or destroyer escorts, periodically rotated from other naval units. Aside from showing the flag, the force presumably gathers local intelligence, represents a tripwire to ward off the improbable contingency of Soviet intervention, and may help to buffer conflicts between local actors. The government of Bahrain has called for U.S. withdrawal by June, 1977, but there remains some uncertainty about the constancy of its position on the U.S. presence.

Just beyond the mouth of the gulf, on the Omani-owned island of Masirah, the British have been operating an air base capable of handling heavy bombers and the long-range P-3 Orion reconnaissance plane. Given the close defense cooperation between the United Kingdom and the United States, one may assume Masirah's availability to the latter on an informal basis as needed. However, with the British no longer able to mind the shop, the United States is now seeking to formalize its access through an agreement with the Omani sultan. That gentleman, a client jointly of the British and the Iranians, who have sustained him in a harsh struggle with tribal insurgents supported by the South Yemenis, is likely to be accommodating.

If it felt the need, the United States could also pick up the Royal Air Force staging base on Gan in the Maldive Islands. The ocean boasts yet a third British-controlled air field, this one on Mahe in the Seychelles, where the United States has a radar tracking station. Mahe also has harbor facilities susceptible to elaboration for military purposes. It appears, however, that the elected government of this British dependency on the edge of independence would not be receptive to the establishment of a Western base.

Down at the Cape of Good Hope, Britain and South Africa share the modern naval base at Simonstown. National poverty is finally accomplishing what Britain's conscience constituency never quite managed, namely, getting the United Kingdom out. Its departure will in no way affect the open invitation to the United States and other NATO countries to use South African facilities and to cooperate with the growing South African coastal defense force.

At the juncture of the Indian Ocean and the Red Sea, there is Djibouti. With an excellent harbor, superior communications, and a well-developed airfield, it has become the *point d'appui* of French naval operations in the Indian Ocean.

Nothing in the recent behavior of the French government, particularly its essentially sterile effort to cultivate a special relationship with the Arab states, augurs Djibouti's availability for any contingency involving U.S. intervention in the Middle East. Transfer even of a rather nominal sovereignty to the largely Muslim inhabitants of the colony would only enhance the already formidable restraints on U.S. use for a Middle East operation in support of Israel, in response to an oil embargo, or for any other purpose hostile to Arab interests. It would not, however, exclude U.S. use of Djibouti in case of a Soviet threat to the oil lanes, a danger sometimes invoked by enthusiasts for a heightened U.S. naval presence in the Indian Ocean.

Ethiopia's recent relinquishment of claims to Djibouti, its coincident determination to prevent a Somali occupation, and the acute financial dependence of the port and its surrounding territory on French budgetary subventions and port-related expenditures presage eventual "independence" under French tutelage, the kind of cozy arrangement that has served the French so satisfactorily in most of West Africa.

Whether France will survive very long on the Horn is increasingly doubtful. The French Left, buoyant with growing electoral support, has called for retirement from this expensive little relic of colonialism. On the Right, that venerable champion of France's imperial mission on the Horn, Pierre Messmer, now declares Djibouti's irrelevance to France's security needs. There are reports that French forces are already being thinned out. If they begin to take casualties from Somali infiltrators, whether before or after a nominal independence for the territory, pressure within France for a complete withdrawal will accumulate rapidly.

The French government will probably be constrained not only by the certain unpopularity of a colonial conflict but also by Somali membership in the Arab League, plus the conspicuous Russian presence not far from the border. Unable to strike at and eliminate the source of guerrilla attacks on the railroad and their forces, the French might well withdraw rather than suffer progressive leakage of blood and treasure. With the patent flagging of French commitment coinciding with the pronounced deterioration of the authority and power of Ethiopia's central government, are the Somalis—now experiencing a hitherto unknown degree of internal cohesion, military strength, and external support—likely to remain quiescent?*

*The SDR's refusal to support an Ethiopian initiative, adopted at the 1976 OAU meeting of heads of state, committing member states, in advance of the TFAI's independence, to respect that independence at least suggests determination to keep all options open.

A Soviet Blockade?

The threat of a Soviet blockade, heralded by Western tocsin ringers and the South African lobby, is credible if one accepts two propositions: first, that with their present or foreseeably available naval resources, the Russians might conceivably spring an effective blockade outside the context of general war between the East and the West; and, second, that an Indian Ocean blockade is a cost-effective way of threatening the West's oil line. The first proposition is simply implausible. The second enjoys a comparable credibility.

The West has the resources to crack a blockade well before it could seriously threaten European and Japanese oil reserves, which could be supplemented on an emergency basis by off-take from West African and Western Hemisphere production. The large current excess capacity in the world's tanker fleet assures the transport flexibility required to effect a temporary change in source. Meanwhile, a normally heterogeneous agglomeration of states with a profound interest in the unimpeded flow of Persian Gulf oil would coalesce to attack the Soviet blockaders. Western air and sea power, operating from the various bases enumerated above and from the several carriers that could be deployed rapidly by the United States, would be supplemented by the increasingly potent Iranian and, probably, Saudi air forces.

The Russians, on the other hand, would fight alone. Air strikes would immediately eliminate their Somali facilities. Arab hostility as well as the Suez Canal's extreme vulnerability would preclude use of the Somali base by the Soviets for the movement of reinforcements or for withdrawal of already damaged Indian Ocean units. Contingents from the Soviet Pacific fleet could be blocked by its U.S. counterpart. Since a blockade could easily escalate to general war, the presence of a substantial proportion of the Soviet Navy in the Indian Ocean rather than in the approaches to the Soviet Union would constitute inconceivable strategic folly. In other words, unless they were to obtain a large quantitative and qualitative advantage in naval combat vessels over the Western navies (a contingency for which there is no present prospect and one well within U.S. capacity to avert), the Russians, if contemplating a blockade, would face an insoluble dilemma.

The long and short of the matter is that, with grossly inadequate air cover, no capacity for rapid reinforcement, and no hope of posing the kind of threat to Western interests which could conceivably evoke panic-stricken political concessions, the Soviets must be presumed willing to take on the combined air and naval might of the Western and Arab states, launched from a rich and widely diffused base structure.

Assuming the Soviet leadership should suddenly seek the direct confrontation it has generally eschewed, there are more efficient and less strategically perilous means for interdicting Persian Gulf oil. The most obviously efficient means is an air attack on the oil fields themselves, launched from Russian bases. A single day's raid could cripple production for months at lilliputian cost compared to the expenditure required to sustain a naval blockade. Despite anticipated exponential upgrading of Saudi and Iranian air defense capabilities, the Russians can still sustain the air-strike option at far less cost than a projected interdiction campaign demands.

Another possibility is sabotage at the source. The large alien population required by the gulf states to operate the fields virtually precludes effective security measures.

A third possibility is naval interdiction in the Mediterranean and the North Atlantic. There would be numerous advantages over an Indian Ocean exercise: vastly superior air cover, short supply lines, nearby reinforcements, ready access to repair facilities, and the capacity to shift missions from interdiction to strategic defense without any significant time lapse.

In addition to its relative inefficiency, an Indian Ocean blockade, initiated before the outbreak of full-scale war between the Soviet and Western blocs, would be extraordinarily perilous. Freedom of passage is a nonnegotiable issue. This must be apparent to the Soviet leadership. Since Western acquiescence would be incredible, initiation of a blockade might be interpreted in Western capitals not as a probe but rather as a prelude to an attack in the European theater. The temptation, then, would be to essay a preemptive, disarming thrust against the various Soviet fleets.

For all of the above reasons, an Indian Ocean blockade would be strategic folly of the highest order. The Russians do not evince any temptation to flirt with this folly. If they envisioned an assault on the sea lanes either as an attractive option for coercion short of total war or as an important adjunct to a conventional war in Europe,* surely they would be turning out large numbers of cheap submarines bedizened with clusters of torpedoes. What they are actually doing each year is building a few very expensive and very sophisticated submarines.[3] They are fairly evenly divided between those that are ideally configured for attacks on carriers and those clearly designed to hunt down and kill missile-

---

* The Soviet forces in central Europe are deployed and equipped for a blitzkrieg, not a prolonged war with the NATO forces opposite them. Western Europe already possesses a six-month oil reserve which, if war broke out, could easily be stretched.

launching submarines. The evident concern to which this construction program responds is nuclear attack on the Soviet heartland.

A Plausible Threat to Western Interests?

While the blockade threat is implausible, is there any way in which an armed Soviet naval presence in the Indian Ocean could, in fact, imperil Western interests? An affirmative response seems implicit both in the sometimes frenzied press campaign to highlight the Soviet presence and also in the West's efforts over the years to preserve and strengthen the conservative regimes that dominate the Persian Gulf.

Soviet naval power is apparently linked in the minds of certain Western strategists with two distinct threats. One is the replacement of existing governments by leftists. The other is an oil embargo by the existing regimes. At first glance, their perceived coexistence is anomalous, even illogical. If conservative regimes may be prepared to employ the oil weapon once again, why any distinct concern for the behavior of radical ones?

The process of eliminating the Western concessions is already well advanced under the conservatives. And there is no correlation between the pace of oil nationalization in a given country and the ideological bent of its ruling elite. The conservative Kuwaitis, for instance, have gone all the way, while the radical Libyans apparently prefer to retain several Western companies as concessionaires. Governments differ not on whether but rather on how best to cook the Western goose. In this connection, the relevant ideology is nationalism, and the conservatives are no less its devotees than their radical counterparts.

States with low reserves and large current revenue needs press hardest for higher prices. Here too, then, neither Marxism nor the Islamic socialism propounded by Libya's Colonel Qaddafi seems to add anything to the West's burdens.

Are radicals more likely than conservatives to employ oil as a political weapon? Quite possibly not. Both gulf traditionalists and radicals generally detest the existence of an Israeli state. Nevertheless, there are two distinctions which make leftist elites appear somewhat more ominous.

Presumably, the first priority of the traditionalists, like other governing elites, is not to rid the Arab world of the Jewish state but rather to maintain themselves as masters in their own states. Since the United States appears organically hostile to radicals and, in any event, has consistently demonstrated its commitment to the Middle East status quo, it presents itself as the only great power on whom the conservatives can rely against internal and external threats. The one act calculated to shake the de facto alliance with the United States is a serious embargo. Hence, on grounds of self-preservation, the traditionalists seem less likely than their radical successors to employ oil as a political weapon.

Traditionalists and radicals may differ in another respect relevant to Western interests in a regular flow of oil and the related question of Arab acceptance of a Jewish state. The kings and sheikhs on the Arab side of the gulf show few signs of enthusiasm for a political nationalism which transcends their respective domains. By contrast, at least some radicals profess commitment to a nationalism as wide as the Arab world. Israel is incompatible with the broader conception of the fatherlands; it is an intolerable alien intrusion. There is, therefore, no basis for peaceful coexistence. If the gulf states were all controlled by Colonel Qaddafis who behaved in a manner consistent with the principles professed before their accessions to power, subsidies would presumably flow only to a militant Egypt. Threatened with the loss of gulf money, Egypt might end its gradual movement toward accommodation.

If the fragile peace shatters, the West could be faced with the alternatives of another oil embargo or the rejection of any commitment to Israeli survival. And if it inclined to the latter alternative, the Israelis *in extremis* could counter by threatening a strike against Arab oil facilities.

Preservation of the conservative regimes also serves Western interests, it has been argued, because the monarchs' sense of a common enemy—the radicals—and their relative freedom from ideological differences help to keep their natural competitive relationships from flaring into violence. If a Qaddafi reigned in Riyadh while the shah endured in Teheran, the risk of violence might be aggravated.

Assuming that the commonality of royal rule does restrain conflict, it does not, however, follow that Western interests would be served by direct or proxy interventions to maintain the existing order. For the effort, particularly where it involves a sally across the gulf by the non-Arab, Muslim schismatics of Persia, could produce, and a good deal more quickly, the very violence for which it was the putative prophylactic.

Any radical nationalists who may be slouching toward Riyadh to assume control do represent some added risk to Western interests in the Middle East. The Soviet naval presence in the Indian Ocean conceivably may enhance the prospect for the overthrow of existing governments on the Arab side of the gulf: Soviet ships might serve as a shield for radical insurgents or some newly installed radical regime threatened with a seaborne intervention mounted by the gulf's counterrevolutionary policeman, the Iranian shah, either alone or in conjunction with Western forces. The risk of direct engagement even with a very modest Soviet tripwire might possibly add a significant element to the deterrent value of Soviet ground forces on the Russo-Iranian border. But, as suggested just above, so might the danger to the oil fields and refineries that an intervention would necessarily incur if they were already under radical control.

The Soviet Navy could also deter a Western thrust against the oil fields themselves in case of an embargo sprung by the present rulers. The possibility of playing an interpositional role deterring the use of Western naval force for Third World interventions has been lost on neither the Soviet nor the American navies. Admiral Gorshkov, commander in chief of the Soviet Navy, has trumpeted it with engaging candor, presumably in the course of the kind of interservice budgetary squabbles so familiar to Pentagon aficionados. For their part, Western navalists have cited it as justification for still greater investments in a surface fleet and a supporting base structure which might allow American ships to reach their target before the Soviet tripwire could be established or, of course, before the Soviets could themselves intervene on behalf of friends.

Policy Implications

The Horn does not hold the key to the future of U.S.-Soviet naval competition in the Indian Ocean. With the distance between Russia's Black Sea base-complex and the Arabian Sea more than halved by the reopening of the Suez Canal,* *peacetime* deployment is feasible for the Soviets without *any* littoral support facilities, albeit with less logistical elegance. Suppose that a joint U.S.-Saudi offer to match Soviet aid could convince the Somalis to end the present invidious hospitality to the air and naval forces of the USSR. Whether the consequent increase in the number of support ships required to maintain combatants would seriously aggravate the financial burden of Indian Ocean patrols is unclear; the cost of constructing and operating additional ships would be partially offset by the elimination of the maintenance costs and the economic and military aid associated with shore facilities.

Loss of access to Somali facilities would not, in fact, reduce the Russians to exclusive reliance on ship-based support. It is extremely unlikely that the United States could influence such littoral states as

---

* From over 7,000 to roughly 3,300 miles.

Mauritius, Mozambique, and the PDRY to close their ports to Soviet ships seeking bunkering, supplies, and minor repairs on strictly commercial terms. One should add that even if all of the littoral states were prepared to succumb to Western financial blandishments (which would inevitably be inflated by Soviet counteroffers), the financial cost to the United States might be no less than the additional costs imposed upon the Soviets by the absence of shore facilities. Both we and they would be poorer. Out-bidding the Russians might be a clever ploy for transferring resources to the Third World; but as a strategy for countering Soviet naval power, it would be unimpressive.

For Soviet fleet missions potentially involving conflict with substantial naval forces, the loss of air-support and missile-testing facilities would be painful and, in the short run, even disastrous. It does not, however, appear that the Russians have any short-run interest in such missions. Their fleet deployment seems to have stabilized at a level below that which the French alone have maintained over the past several years. For the present, they seem interested essentially in gathering such marginal political capital as can putatively be acquired through showing the flag, in developing operational experience, and, possibly, in maintaining a potential tripwire. They may be equally interested in signaling the will and capacity to match any escalation in Western activity. That signal is, of course, best conveyed by shore facilities which can support a much enlarged fleet deployment, as Diego Garcia will support a thrust of U.S. ships into the area.

Facilities in Somalia thus serve a deterrent role as well as facilitating the logistics of contemporary operations and laying a foundation for the option of an enlarged presence. If forced to leave, the Russians would probably seek and, as well, find an alternative site. For at least one of the largely pauperized littoral countries, Soviet largesse would likely prove irresistible. And poverty may not be the only incentive to exchanging a fleet-support quo for Soviet quid.

In southern Africa, there is a rapidly gathering risk of interstate conflict. Both South Africa and Southern Rhodesia have affirmed their intention of hotly pursuing guerrillas across national frontiers. If the United States cannot or will not stop them, the government of Mozambique may feel compelled to trade base rights for Soviet protection. Hence, even if we could, without unacceptable costs, lever the Russians out of Somalia, the resulting strategic gains promise to be short-lived as well as marginal.

With its present naval resources, the Soviet Union has a modest capacity to assist in maintaining or displacing regimes in the countries that spread along the east coast of Africa. This interventionary capacity remains signally inferior to the U.S. forces that can surge into the area and operate with fuel stored on Diego Garcia. So the military means for inhibiting whatever appetite for intervention the Soviets may now possess or soon acquire are well in hand. Whether the end is worth pursuing along the African littoral where, because of the weakness of local forces, the limited Soviet capabilities might prove decisive is less clear.

By any calculation, East and Central Africa are areas of marginal concern to the West. Moreover, the Russians have yet to demonstrate that, outside of the special case of Eastern Europe, they can prevent client regimes from doing business with the West. Even the Somalis, with all their military dependence, have sought to place relations with the United States on a reasonably amicable, businesslike basis. And after all that we did to Indochina, the government of Vietnam is now seeking the return of Western oil companies. In the generality of cases where we have failed to establish constructive relations with radical regimes in the Third World, the fault lies far less in Moscow's Svengalian influence than in Washington's ideological pique. If we stop defining ourselves out of the game, we will find that there are few, if any, cases where we cannot stay in.

Our apparent ability to remain in the game is one reason why two decades of U.S. intervention on behalf of preferred factions in Third World power struggles now seems so grotesquely exorbitant. If, on balance, our essays in intervention have incurred costs out of all proportion to their persuasively arguable benefits, why should we be overly concerned if the Russians try their hand at creating Frankenstein clients? One is often bemused by the self-flagellating assumption of certain Western strategists and the politicians they service that the Russians can squeeze luxurious benefits out of policies our experience inclines us to write off. *Obviously, this is not to say that the United States should treat every Soviet intervention, regardless of circumstances, with indifference.* But we should drop the dangerous presumption that every Soviet intervention is a challenge requiring a resolute response. That belligerent reflex mandates indifference to local equities and balances of power, as well as to degrees of Western and Soviet interest and involvement. It mandates, in other words, just the sort of myopia that has cost us so dearly in the past.

Easily deliverable countervailing naval power is one way of reducing the putative charm of the interventionary prospect. An alternative and less costly approach is agreement, express or implied, on restraint in force deployments. The United States has apparently failed to pursue vigorously the possibility of working out formal reciprocal restraints. In a 1971 speech, Soviet Party Secretary Leonid Brezhnev proposed the negotiation of arms limitations for the Mediterranean *and* the Indian Ocean. The idea failed to arouse any readily apparent U.S. interest. The Russians have made no further public effort to probe Washington's receptivity.

Asymmetries between the interests, strategies, facilities, and weapon systems of the United States and the USSR inhibit if they do not flatly preclude acceptance of limits calculated in identical units of naval and air power. What, for instance, would be the Soviet equivalent of a U.S. nuclear carrier? Would it be two missile-armed cruisers? A squadron of fighter-bombers in Somalia? And so on. What, moreover, can equivalences between discrete weapon systems mean? The answer is that outside the context of particular missions, strategies, and contingencies, each of which may mandate a different "just balance," they mean very little at all.

The Strategic Arms Limitation Talks (SALT) dealt primarily with a single contingency (nuclear war), a single strategy (deterrence), and a single common interest (avoiding nuclear war). They were preceded by years of clarifying analysis and debate. Yet a powerful political impetus flowing from the highest levels of government was required to produce agreements, quickly subjected to unrelenting criticism. Agreement on a table of power equivalents mediating equitably among the asymmetries enumerated above in order to reach agreement on force deployments probably requires transcendance of larger and less well examined conceptual difficulties than those which beset SALT. However, unlike advantages gained through serious errors in the calculus of deterrence, any advantage gained through an agreement on deployment restraints could easily be rectified. Nevertheless, given the public's strategic naivete and the even more complex calculations probably required in this case, such an agreement might be peculiarly vulnerable to the sort of vituperative attack raised against agreements on deterrence.

These obstacles are formidable; no one has claimed that they are insuperable. Inside the government, opposition to an agreement seems to rest on other grounds.

Within the U.S. Navy, formal restraints on deployment appear to be regarded with the sort of unbuttoned enthusiasm one might reserve for a viper slithering into one's bed. This frank hostility is widely shared in the national security bureaucracy and, very likely, in its Soviet counterpart.

Its source is not obscure. People who achieve positions of responsibility in most countries, but particularly in great powers, believe quite simply that the ultimate political arbiter is raw military power and that its demonstrable availability establishes the necessary background against which a state wages an effective diplomacy.

Naval power is seen to have two great virtues: it is easy to exhibit, and it can be employed worldwide and in doses carefully proportioned to the perceived requirements of each case. More precisely, it is by far the most effective means for intervention in the Third World.

As naval power has two great virtues, Indian Ocean deployment limitations would have two great vices: they would create a precedent for limiting deployment in other seas and threaten to erode the credibility of U.S. intervention in the Persian Gulf or in other parts of the littoral.

While defending the appropriation for Diego Garcia, one State Department expert summed up the underlying administration position with fetching candor: "We would want a naval presence in the Indian Ocean," he said, "even if the Russians were not there at all. We have interests there quite independent of our competitive relationship with the Soviets just as they have interests quite unrelated to us." As notional examples of specific contingencies requiring a naval presence, he cited guerrilla attacks on Israeli tankers passing through Bab el Mandeb and the eruption of hostilities between Iran and Iraq in which the United States, the principal armorer of the shah, would intervene to keep the peace.*

Nothing was said about occupying the gulf. But one cannot help suspecting that that is a contingency lurking in some recess of the strategic mind when the virtues of a naval presence are extolled. As I have suggested, it may in fact be a major source of concern for the Soviet naval presence. The specter which may haunt is not an attack on the tankers or even Soviet interventions in the style of the 1965 U.S. occupation of the Dominican Republic but rather Soviet interposition in case the United States chooses this means to shore up the existing international economic order.

A force-limitation agreement might cover the geography as well as the dimensions of naval deployments. It might, for instance, declare the Persian Gulf out of bounds for both navies. That would, of course, leave the local traditionalists with a free hand to defend the status quo. On the other hand, combined with overall force limita-

---

* The case is more paradoxical than incredible. The United States sells for profit and for influence and in the belief that if it does not, others will. The sales are not designed to facilitate Iranian conduct of a belligerent foreign policy, although they may, indeed, have that effect.

tions throughout the Indian Ocean, it would inhibit Western intervention in case of an oil embargo by the existing regimes. And it would have the precedential consequences cited above.

Probably the Russians have never been seriously interested in force-deployment limitations. Apparently we will not try very hard to find out. Why not? First, because it would appear that Secretary Kissinger, ever sensitive to the nuance of national image, fears that a U.S. initiative at this time might be construed as a sign of weakness or of indifference to Soviet activities in Africa. And second, because, despite our disaster in Vietnam, too many people have not quite relinquished the belief that, in our transactions with the Third World, force is only the conduct of diplomacy by other means.

As both State and Defense Department officials have implied, there may already be a tacit understanding on force limitations. The Russians have stabilized the number and types of ships they are regularly deploying in the Indian Ocean. The United States, for its part, has not sent any substantial naval contingent into the area for over a year. Senior officials in Washington have denied publicly any intention of establishing an Indian Ocean fleet. They have defended Diego Garcia only as a means of facilitating occasional patrols and as insurance in case of certain contingencies, including augmented and more-aggressive Soviet operations.

Tacit arrangements are, of course, relatively more vulnerable than formal agreements to evasion through elastic interpretation and to wholesale annulment at the behest of new calculations of interest. Weighted with these generic deficiencies, informal rules of the game are generally even less effective than express understandings in restraining domestic demands for greater military expenditures.

Because their limits tend toward fuzziness and because they provide neither a public obligation nor the machinery to conciliate differences, tacit understandings are, in addition, relatively more likely to produce conflicting interpretations of the arrangement. The danger of conflicting interpretations is particularly acute in the present case where either side may be moved by the enumerated interests unrelated to superpower competition to raise its profile. Still, partially as a consequence of those interests, the prospect of a more articulate understanding seems bleak.

Notes

1. See for example D. R. Cox, "Sea Power and Soviet Foreign Policy," *U.S. Naval Proceedings* 95 (June 1969) : 41 ff; T. B. Millar, "Soviet Policies South and East of Suez," *Foreign Affairs* 52 (October 1973) :73; L. Martin, "The New Power Gap in the Indian Ocean," *Interplay* 3 (January 1969) :37; O. M. Smolansky, "Soviet Entry into the Indian Ocean: An Analysis" in Michael MccGwire, ed., *Soviet Naval Developments* (New York: Praeger, 1973), p. 421.

2. See generally R. G. Weinland, "The Changing Mission of the Soviet Navy," *Survival* 14 (May/June 1972) : 131-2; Geoffrey Jukes, "The Indian Ocean in Soviet Naval Policy," *Adelphi Papers Number Eighty-seven* (London: International Institute of Strategic Studies, 1972), pp. 12-18; A. J. Cottrell and R. M. Burrell, "Soviet-U.S. Naval Competition in the Indian Ocean," *Orbis* 18 (Winter 1975) : 1123.

3. *Jane's Fighting Ships* (New York: Franklin Watts, Inc., 1975-76).

The Geopolitical Context: Eritrea, Israel and the Red Sea 8

The future of Eritrea engages American concern through the medium of Israeli security interests. Some Israeli defense analysts argue that an independent Eritrea will enhance the capacity of the Arab states to blockade or harass commerce passing through the Red Sea and the Gulf of Aden to and from the port of Eilat.[1] The most important item in this rapidly growing stream of goods (since 1967, trade through Eilat has been increasing at a rate of more than fifteen percent annually) is Iranian oil, which, following the return of the Sinai oil fields to Egypt, now assumes even greater significance for the Israeli economy. Iranian oil not only satisfies Israeli energy needs but, in addition, is a source of hard currency: the oil pipeline between Eilat and Ashkelon on Israel's Mediterranean coast is the foundation for a transit trade which by 1972 had reached an annual level of thirty million tons. Several pumping stations under construction will soon permit exploitation of the pipeline's full sixty-million-ton capacity.

The threat of an Arab blockade or lower-order forms of harassment links up with U.S. interests in at least two ways. First, as a state committed to Israel's survival, the United States is concerned about any threat to Israel's economy, logistics, or morale. Second, as a consumer of Arab oil and an ally of states far more dependent on the uninterrupted flow of oil from the Middle East, it is concerned about any spark which could reignite the Middle East conflict. It is similarly concerned about risks to the security of the tanker fleet moving Persian Gulf oil to Western markets.

The Dual Threats

Although some Israeli and American analysts speak broadly of an "Arab threat," in fact there are two quite distinct threats to Israeli commerce. The main threat is posed by the Arab states, principally Egypt and Saudi Arabia, since only they have at their disposition substantial naval forces and air power in the Red Sea area. Non-state actors — either some faction of the Palestine Liberation Organization or, under certain conceivable circumstances, of the Eritrean Liberation Movement constitute a second, albeit minor, threat with distinctly different political, strategic and tactical constraints.

Each threat has materialized once. The guerrillas struck in 1971. Although the details remain rather obscure, it appears that a Palestinian commando unit attacked the Israeli tanker *Coral Sea* as it was passing through the Strait of Bab el Mandeb. The attack was launched from the island of Perim. Part of the territory of the People's Democratic Republic of Yemen (PDRY), Perim squats in the strait about sixteen miles from the African coast. The leading Israeli authority on the Horn, Dr. Mordechai Abir, alleges that "some of the PDRY leaders colluded in this gambit."[2]

The Egyptian blockade threat assumed tangible form in 1973 as a short-lived incident of the October war. It was instituted unofficially, not contested by the Israelis, and quietly lifted at the time, and probably as one condition, of the cease-fire.

EGYPT WITH A LITTLE HELP FROM ITS FRIENDS

Although Egypt would seem to be the Arab state with the most-compelling interest in a southern blockade beyond the range of Israeli hegemony in the air and at sea, until 1973 it evinced peculiarly little interest in developments around the Strait of Bab el Mandeb. For instance, it was one of the few Arab states not even accused of assisting the Eritrean insurgency.

With Egypt very much in the background as, at best, a potential collaborator, the southern strategy was noisily promoted by Libya and the PDRY. The former emerged as the main source of arms for the Eritreans, while the latter allowed its shoreline to be used as an entrepôt and transshipment point for arms provided by Libya and possibly by Syria and Iraq as well.

Egyptian passivity may have been attributable to a variety of factors: the intense strain on its military and economic resources, the stresses created by the mass expulsion of Soviet advisers, the need to build up its military potential along the Suez Canal, the long-term effort to cultivate the black African states who were certain to resent support of any separatist movement, and an acute appreciation of Israeli sensitivity to a blockade and Egypt's grave vulnerability to Israeli countermeasures.

There is another or additional explanation, namely, a conviction in Cairo that access to air and naval facilities along the

Eritrean coast would not significantly enhance its ability to harass or wholly to halt Israeli commerce. Whatever their differences with Cairo on other issues, when it comes to the matter of Israel, the governments of the Sudan, Saudi Arabia, the two Yemens, and the Somali Democratic Republic are at least as likely as the government of an independent Eritrea to lend needed military support. The PDRY alone disposes of the island of Perim (on which by 1972 it had already begun to place artillery facing the strait*), the former British naval base in Aden, and an airfield. North Yemen also had a port (Hodeida) and an airfield. With these potentially available facilities on both sides and in the very mouth of the strait, plus Sudanese and Saudi facilities farther north and the Somali port of Berbera south of Bab el Mandeb, the Eritrean ports of Massawa and Assab and the air base at Asmara could not have seemed much more than redundant, particularly in light of the air and naval forces the Egyptians and their allies were able to deploy. In fact, existing facilities were adequate to support the 1973 blockade. And, having at the Rabat conference in 1974 negotiated under the aegis of the Arab League a ninety-nine-year lease of Perim Island from the PDRY, Egypt is now in a position to strengthen the blockade infrastructure.**

From a strictly military point of view, therefore, Eritrea should not be a particularly tempting target of opportunity for the Arab states. Its significance lies not in the ways it can help but in the way it can hurt the Arab cause. Rather than being an opportunity, it is a threat. For while the Arabs are so well endowed in the area as to justify indifference to Eritrean facilities, the Israelis, on the other hand, have nothing at all. For them, acquisition of military facilities in Eritrea would be a menacing counterstroke.

Even for the Israelis, however, military facilities in Eritrea may not be an absolutely essential condition of a credible blockade-smashing strategy. Having acquired ˌan inflight refueling capability, the Israeli Air Force can strike at targets well beyond Bab el Mandeb and Aden with fighter-bombers launched from Israeli soil. Its planes may also be able to provide some cover for the long-range missile boats which during the 1973 war dominated the Syrian and Egyptian navies in the Mediterranean. Israeli experts have hinted that, given the proper air cover, a flotilla of these boats, based at Sharm el Sheikh, could challenge a blockade mounted at Bab el Mandeb. The effort could not be made in 1973 because the few

---

*The artillery consisted, however, of nothing more than a few immobilized tanks.

**By mid-1976, it apparently had not made any effort to do so.

boats then available were deployed in the Mediterranean and, moreover, the Israeli Air Force was entirely engaged in the main struggle along Israel's borders.

While Eritrean bases may not be an absolutely necessary condition for the direct defense of Israeli shipping in the southern Red Sea and the Gulf of Aden, their potential contribution to such an effort is not questioned. It is, for instance, doubtful that aerial refueling would permit the sustained air cover without which the missile boats would be dangerously exposed. Moreover, even if the boats could reach their destination and successfully engage a flotilla of blockading ships, there is no sign of an existing Israeli capability to maintain these ships for sustained combat and patrol far from shore facilities. Thus, the blockaders might be able to avoid combat while the Israeli missile boats were in the area and then return to their mission once the boats had withdrawn.

The growing dialogue over the strategic significance of Sharm el Sheikh indirectly supports these doubts. In responding to the Egyptian claim that Sharm el Sheikh is not essential to Israeli security because the Arabs can achieve the same strangulating effect by blockading the southern strait as it can by blocking the Strait of Tiran, Israel, although referring *en passant* to the possibility of attacking a southern blockade from its base at Sharm el Sheikh, has primarily emphasized *deterrent* measures which it could employ against Arab commerce in the Gulf of Suez and the northern part of the Red Sea.

The Arab states have not been insensitive to the risk of an Israeli redoubt within easy striking distance of Bab el Mandeb. Following the quiet increase in Israeli military assistance to the Ethiopian government which coincided with the 1971 visit to Ethiopia of General Bar-Lev, the Israeli chief of staff, the Arab press began reporting the construction of Israeli naval and air bases on tiny Ethiopian-controlled islands near the strait. The reports appear to have been entirely unfounded and may be understood as part of a prophylactic effort to marshal Arab and African opposition to an Ethiopian-Israeli base deal. The intense Arab-orchestrated pressure for a rupture of relations with Israel exerted against Haile Selassie through the medium of the Organization of African Unity (OAU) may also have been a facet of a conscious policy of barring an Israeli military presence on the southern coast.

The potential negative contribution of Eritrean facilities to the Arabs' southern strategy may also explain Egypt's show of indifference to the Eritrean Liberation Movement, for the one thing calculated to drive the cautious Emperor to an open alliance with the Israelis would have been a uniform and categorical Arab commitment to the secessionists. Egyptian and, for that matter, Saudi Arabian reticence gave the Emperor a continuing incentive for neutrality in the Arab-Israeli conflict.

As far as one can tell, the Israeli government never sounded out its Ethiopian counterpart about the possibility of a base-rights agreement. In the late 1960s, an Eritrean base may have seemed a relative indulgence, for at that point the United States still appeared to have a long-term interest in maintaining Kagnew Station, its own huge military-communications and intelligence-monitoring installation near Asmara. With the Suez Canal closed, Kagnew was serviced primarily by ships passing through Bab el Mandeb to the port of Massawa. Israel could therefore rely on the U.S. interest in an open and secure route through the strait. But by the early 1970s, a Pentagon decision to phase out Kagnew became evident. Satellites had made part of Kagnew's operations redundant. The remainder could be transferred to Diego Garcia which, being an uninhabited island under British sovereignty, provided a far more secure setting. Washington's coincident refusal to respond affirmatively to the Emperor's pleas for a major step-up in arms aid to counter the expanded Soviet assistance to the Somali armed forces not only confirmed the first signs of Kagnew's fate but in addition signaled Washington's indifference to any alternative U.S. military enterprise (for example, a staging base for intervention in East Africa and the Middle East) on the Eritrean coast.

These events, coupled with the attack on the *Coral Sea,* the fortification of Perim, the growing Russian presence in Somalia, and the continued though uneven progress of the Eritrean insurgents, quickened Israeli concern. Israel responded by expanding economic development and military assistance programs for Ethiopia. The Israeli government was not, however, willing to draw sophisticated weapons out of its own limited inventories in order to satisfy Ethiopian desires for force modernization.

THE GUERRILLAS

Access to shore facilities with intimate proximity to the Bab el Mandeb choke point is not essential to a state like Egypt (which disposes of submarines, destroyers, and bombers) ; to the guerillas, who would, at best, rely on small, lightly armed boats and rockets with an effective range of only a few miles, it is critical.

The PDRY's decision to lease Perim Island to Egypt enhanced the value of the Eritrean coast to the Palestine Liberation Organization as a possible launch point for operations against Israeli commerce. Indeed, if, as appears likely, the lease reflects the Aden government's willingness to subordinate its own conceptions of an

appropriate southern strategy to those of the generally more prudent men in Cairo and Riyadh, Eritrea is the *only* place left to the
guerrillas. Being Ethiopian territory, it cannot be policed by the
Egyptians. And given the terribly stretched resources of the Ethiopians, their control is not much better than nominal. As it is, they
are unable to prevent small boats from slipping back and forth between the Arabian and African coasts with arms for the Eritrean
Liberation Movement.

The Options in Eritrea

THE WAR GOES ON

Assuming that the Palestinians can no longer rely on assistance
from the PDRY, it is hard to see how they could deploy weapons
along the littoral without the collaboration of the Eritrean insurgents. Social revolutionaries within the liberation movements might
be willing, on ideological grounds alone, to assist a radical splinter
of the Palestinian coalition, like the followers of George Habash.
For the moment, however, prudence should incline the bulk of the
movements toward a policy of noncooperation, indeed of active opposition.

Why? Because the insurgents already have demonstrated that,
without a major new increment of external support, the Ethiopian
armed forces cannot do more than cling to the major cities and
towns at ever increasing cost to and strain on the central government in Addis Ababa. And that strategic posture is unfavorable
enough to the Dergue to give their Eritrean adversaries the prospect
of ultimate victory.

The Eritreans are not insensitive to U.S. concern for the security
of Western and Israeli commerce in the Red Sea. In 1974, while
Washington was considering the Dergue's request for immediate
delivery of $30 million worth of arms and ammunition, Eritrean
leaders threatened to attack Israeli vessels passing along the coast if
the request were granted. We do not know whether the subsequent
failure to carry out that threat can be attributed, in part or in
whole, to Washington's temporizing authorization of only $7 mil-
lion in sales. Pressure from Arab governments to avoid any action
which could threaten the Middle East cease-fire or the tactical constraints imposed by confrontation with reinforced elements of the
Ethiopian army may have been decisive. What we should know is
that a policy of active support of the Ethiopian government's
counterinsurgency efforts risks calling into being the very contingency invoked by some Western analysts to justify that support.

There is no nicely illuminated threshold above which the delivery of U.S. arms to Ethiopia would trigger Eritrean retaliation. If victory for the Eritreans is delayed very much longer, their anger over existing levels of U.S. support for Ethiopia may overcome the restraint they have so far exercised in the knowledge that provocative actions on their part could generate augmented U.S. support for the Dergue.

AN INDEPENDENT ERITREA

Even a fairly gradual withdrawal of U.S. assistance might erode the central government's capacity to maintain its tenuous grip on Eritrea. Withdrawal could, in other words, foster the birth of an independent state. The population of the new state would be very evenly divided between the Christian and Muslim faiths. Although Muslims have been numerically predominant in the liberation movements, there are Christians in the leadership of both the Eritrean Liberation Front and the allegedly more radical Popular Liberation Forces. Moreover, Christians undoubtedly formed a majority among the former police officers and students who flocked to join the rebels during and after the insurgent offensive in the fall of 1974. Opposition to the central government now seems equally intense among Christians and Muslims.

Collaboration in the struggle for independence, following in the footsteps of parliamentary collaboration during the brief democratic honeymoon which preceded Haile Selassie's gutting of the province's original automony, presages (although it by no means assures) communal balance within a postindependence regime. If Christians do secure a major share of power, like their confessional counterparts in Lebanon they will naturally be reluctant to support foreign policy initiatives calculated to plant in their midst the armed forces of Muslim Arab states. Of course, Christians may not acquire an effective veto. Or, for need of petrodollars and for fear of Ethiopian revanche, they may decline to exercise it. There is, therefore, no guarantee that the government of an independent Eritrea will not offer base rights to Israel's main opponents. But for the reasons elaborated above, nothing of great strategic significance will have been lost, even on the assumption that the Arabs are, in fact, likely to attempt a blockade.

With the opening of the Suez Canal, that assumption has lost most of its plausibility. In the first place, Western interests in the security of the canal route will inhibit an Arab threat to free passage. Although Israeli commerce would be the only target, interdiction operations—checking of documents and cargoes, as well as battles between blockaders and armed Israeli merchant and convoying missile ships — would inevitably affect all commerce.

Second, the Russians would be concerned about threats to passage. As noted earlier, the Indian Ocean is an important area of operations for their vast fishing fleets. And the Red Sea will normally be more efficient for the carriage of goods to major trading partners like India and to the Asiatic coast of the Soviet Union. Beyond those immediate practical considerations, the Soviet Union, as an emergent sea power, has acquired a powerful interest in the principle of free passage through international straits. Like the United States, it has insisted at the Law of the Sea Conference that no enlarged definition of a nation's territorial sea will be recognized unless free passage through and over traditionally international straits is conceded. Israeli strategists are probably right, therefore, in believing that, with the canal now open, a blockade of Bab el Mandeb is unlikely except in the context of all-out war ignited by events nearer the center of the storm. A manifest U.S. capacity and, far more important, will to challenge obstacles to free passage, other than in the event of a major war, would further reduce the likelihood of strait-blocking activities by the Egyptians or some other Arab government.

In that case, one may ask, why are the Arab states paying the PDRY $150 million for a ninety-nine-year lease on Perim Island? Doesn't that imply a considerably greater willingness to employ the blockade option than the preceding analysis suggests? Not necessarily. There remains, after all, the danger of a full-scale renewal of the conflict. In addition, despite Israeli resistance to the idea, the manifest threat of a blockade at or near Bab el Mandeb does somewhat weaken the force of the security argument for permanent Israeli control of Sharm el Sheikh. Furthermore, from their base on Perim Island, the Egyptians can police action by the PDRY or by guerrilla groups whose sense of timing or the appropriateness of risks may not coincide with strategy forged in Cairo, Damascus, and Riyadh. Finally, the lease may have been designed to deny Soviet access to the island.

While it would not be remarkable for the government of an independent Eritrea to associate itself with the major Arab states, its toleration of military operations launched from its soil by Palestinian commando units would be astounding. Such tolerance would alienate both Egypt and the major dispensers of petrodollars, with the possible exception of Libya. It would invite Israeli retaliation against the country's two most important assets: the ports of Assab and Massawa. The mere threat of Eritrean involvement in any kind of armed conflict would deflect commercial shipping and hence transit trade from the interior to the competing port of Djibouti.

In addition to having every incentive to preclude use of its territory for guerrilla activities, an Eritrean government should be better placed than its embattled Ethiopian counterpart to exercise effective control over the coast, since it should enjoy amicable relations with the PDRY.

A NEGOTIATED SETTLEMENT

A negotiated settlement would insure denial of the coast to Arab governments, as well as guerrillas, because the minimum conditions of a settlement conceivably acceptable to any foreseeable Ethiopian government are neutralization of Eritrea and assured Ethiopian access to the Red Sea. The former condition, whether guaranteed by Ethiopia's retention of a veto over certain policies of an autonomous but loosely federated Eritrean state or by some other arrangement, would preclude any alien military presence. The latter could be effectively guaranteed only if Ethiopia retained or, at worst, shared sovereignty over the southern port of Assab and a land corridor running to it from the highlands. Ethiopian control of Assab would not only physically block Arab use of the coast at the narrow threshold of Bab el Mandeb but in addition would provide the Ethiopians with the port facilities and the consequent incentive for keeping the area clear of irregular forces that could jeopardize commerce.

The fact that Eritrea's neutralization would also deny Israel access to facilities along the coast should not dull the attractions of a negotiated settlement, for it is hard to envision any plausible conjunction of circumstances which could produce a usable Israeli base.

Were the Ethiopians to offer Israel base rights today, they would have to anticipate a qualitative jump in Arab support for the Eritreans and would certainly risk some form of direct Arab intervention. Arab, and particularly Egyptian, support — hitherto muted — of Somali claims could be expected to intensify. A base deal would, in addition, reinvigorate the campaign led originally by Libya to force the withdrawal of the headquarters of the OAU from Addis.

Aside from these immediate consequences, an Ethiopian-Israeli alliance would guarantee long-term enmity between Ethiopia and the renascent Arab states, whose African kin border Ethiopia on three sides. This could, in turn, complicate the Dergue's efforts to assimilate into the main stream of Ethiopian nationalism the thirty-five to forty percent of the population which professes the Muslim faith.

And what can the Israelis offer in return? They do not have sufficient naval resources to block the passage of arms across the Red
Sea, arms which could in any event continue to cross the immense
border Ethiopia shares with the Sudan. The Israelis cannot spare
substantial manpower to assist in the pacification of Eritrea. And if
they could not find spare weapons for Ethiopia before the October
war at a time of supreme military self-confidence, they are hardly
likely to find them today. Hence, Uncle Sam would have to provide
the weapons which might conceivably induce the Ethiopians to
lease base rights.

Whether arms aid came from Jerusalem or Washington, its effect, as noted earlier, would be the same: it would identify both
countries as the direct antagonists of Eritrean independence with
the clear danger that that identification entails. And even if one
could assume that the Ethiopians can be bought with arms and that
the United States is willing to intensify its pro-Israeli tilt (and thus
reduce its credibiltiy as a Middle East broker) by providing
Ethiopia with the necessary compensation, the buying would not
achieve its objective.

To be useful, military facilities must be secure. That is one of
the reasons for the rapid phase-out of Kagnew in the face of crescendoing conflict in Eritrea. The Ethiopian army, whatever the
new gadgets with which it might be equipped, could not provide
that security, at least in the near term. At best, it would maintain
its grip on a few fixed points. The guerrillas, aided by an ever more
sympathetic population, would continue to infiltrate Ethiopian
strongholds and, armed by Arab states, would lob ordnance onto
Israeli base facilities.

In short, a hard look at the real world makes the option of an
Israeli base seem illusory. And even if it were not, there is at least
some question whether Israel's strategic interests would be served
optimally by the necessary dispersal of its naval and air forces to the
Eritrean coast. As the last round of war demonstrated, both sides
burn up ordnance at a rate demanding fairly rapid resupply by
superpower patrons. The latter will continue to have powerful
vested interests in capping a gusher of violence. Hence, a protracted
Middle East conflict is virtually inconceivable. But it is only in case
of protracted conflict that a blockade of Israeli shipping could
achieve significant impact.

The Israelis can deter a blockade or lesser forms of harassment
by puissant means well within their present capabilities. These include harassment of Egyptian oil operations in Sinai and the Gulf of
Suez and attacks on the tanker fleet the Arab states are now beginning to acquire. Furthermore, even very low levels of retaliatory vio-

lence in the area of the canal and its approaches would suffice to dry up the stream of commerce which once again eases Egypt's perennially dreadful financial constraints. A halt in canal traffic would also have severe consequences for the PDRY if, as is likely, Aden reacquires some portion of its earlier prominence as a canal-route port.

The essence of the matter, then, is that within the larger strategic context of Arab-Israeli relations, Israeli strangulation at the so-called choke point of Bab el Mandeb is not a plausible contingency.

Notes

1. See for example, Mordechai Abir, "Red Sea Politics," *Adelphi Papers Number Ninety-three* (London: International Institute of Strategic Studies, 1972), pp. 30-7.

2. Mordechai Abir, "Sharm al-Sheikh — Bab al-Mandeb: The Strategic Balance and Israel's Southern Approaches," *Jerusalem Papers on Peace Problems* (Jerusalem: The Hebrew University, 1974), p. 13.

Peaceful Settlement on the Horn: The Margin of Policy

Eritrea

In the summer of 1976, as this book goes to press, the Eritrean war continues on its murderous course. The human and economic damage to Eritrea is incalculable. Shooting, bombing, and, where possible, starving the Eritrean people, the Ethiopian government dissipates the slim resources of manpower, imagination, and capital available to manage the vast social revolution it has set in motion elsewhere in the country.

Outsiders, far from the scene and untouched by its bloody passions, can easily envision compromises that respect in large measure the main functional concerns of both antagonists. The essential features of a conceivable settlement are not obscure. The Eritreans must be assured an autonomy that the Ethiopians cannot eviscerate at will. Eritrea must not, in other words, be vulnerable to shifts in Ethiopian preference or personnel. The Ethiopians, for their part, require assured access to the sea, a guarantee that Eritrea will not become a launching pad for an assault on the highlands, and some means of avoiding any broadly applicable precedent for secession. The current orthodoxy in international relations which postulates absolute sovereignty as the only completely satisfactory expression of nationalist aspirations makes these interests incompatible. Either the parties must transcend the conventional architecture of sovereignty or resign themselves to endless and mutually ruinous conflict.

Transcendance can be achieved only through external involvement. The Eritreans have already been betrayed once. Hence, even if they could put aside their understandable rage at everything they have suffered, they could not accept anything short of unqualified autonomy unless externally guaranteed neutrality were substituted for the normal means of self-protection – including military alliance with more powerful states — available to an independent nation. The guarantors of Eritrean autonomy and neutrality could coincidentally undertake to assure Ethiopian access to the Red Sea ports, a necessary condition of any negotiated settlement.

In light of Eritrea's constitutional history, the United Nations is a natural candidate for the role of guarantor. The paramount advantage of recourse to the United Nations is the emphasis thereby placed on the unique character of this case. As the Eritreans have argued often and well, this is not another instance of attempted revision of colonial boundaries. This is not Biafra, Katanga, or, for that matter, the Ogaden. Eritrea was a self-contained colonial unit and therefore can itself rely on the principle of the sanctity of colonial boundaries which is holy writ in the Third World, above all in Africa. It can, moreover, rest its claims on the unique fact of a General Assembly resolution granting it local autonomy. Breach of that resolution entitles it to seek review of the original arrangement. And since the violation of Ethiopia's obligations under that resolution was effected by the *ancien régime,* the revolutionary government in Addis, by focusing blame on the Emperor, can moderate embarrassment incident to its accepting this plea for a revised relationship between the two states and a reassertion of General Assembly jurisdiction.

There are variations on this essential conception which might seem more satisfactory to the parties. For instance, the General Assembly could delegate its supervisory responsibilities to the Organization of African Unity or to a select group of member states acceptable to both the Eritreans and the Ethiopian Dergue. Further, to assure compliance and to mediate any disputes which might arise in interpreting the agreement, the secretary-general could appoint a personal representative who would be permanently resident in Eritrea. Moreover, during the touchy and critical period following negotiation of a settlement, implementation could be supervised by a United Nations force drawn from states acceptable to the parties.

The dangerous question of sovereignty could be waffled. Formally, the relationship between Eritrea and Ethiopia might be federal. Following the precedent of the Ukraine and Byelorussia, Eritrea could be admitted to United Nations membership. The parties might agree to joint embassies in important foreign countries. They might also agree to require the ambassadors of all foreign states to be accredited to the two federation capitals.

By employing these reasonable means for confusing the issue of sovereignty and by emphasizing the unique features of the Eritrean case, Ethiopia could grant Eritrea the substance of an independent national life without exposing itself to a potentially unraveling precedent. Indeed, if, in the course of negotiating a settlement, the Ethiopians secured from the Eritreans and from the General Assembly a reaffirmation of the integrity of the boundaries inherited from the colonial era, their position vis-à-vis the Somalis could only be strengthened.

Although it is therefore possible to envision a settlement responsive to the central functional concerns of Eritreans and Ethiopians, without the catalyst of a major diplomatic initiative from outside the Horn they may remain locked indefinitely in their terrible stalemate. The obvious, perhaps the only possible, authors of such an initiative are the principal supporters of the two contestants, the United States and the Arab countries. Only they, acting in close concert, can orchestrate the blend of promised benefits and threatened deprivations that might conceivably force both sides to moderate their maximalist positions and explore unconventional solutions to their presently irreconcilable claims.

The initiative must include a specific set of proposals, for clearly it is not enough to get the parties to the negotiating table. Once seated, they must be tempted or coerced, as necessary, to break through the profound emotional and intellectual obstacles to compromise. Specific proposals are required both to reorient their thinking and to provide an enforceable test of good faith. It must be clear to the parties that their patrons are already agreed on the parameters of a reasonable solution and are prepared to act collectively to punish intransigence and to reward moderation. The main sanction would be the withdrawal of military assistance. The tendered benefits would include large-scale economic assistance and support for the long-term integrity of a negotiated solution.

Quite possibly, a number of Arab states will resist any effort to force the Eritreans to accept something less than full independence. But if my analysis of the strategic situation is accurate, neutralization of the Eritrean coast will appeal to the leading Arab governments, particularly to the Cairo-Riyadh axis and its associated states, who are, after all, the most interested parties as well as those deploying the most relevant military and financial assets.

Whatever diplomatic initiatives the U.S. government has attempted thus far have been off-hand, half-hearted, and insufficiently nourished by sensitivity to the equities of the parties and their fundamental requirements for a peaceful settlement. Washington's principal contribution to peace on the Horn has been a marked acceleration of military assistance to the Ethiopian armed forces—from a total of $23.9 million in fiscal year 1974 to $37.6 million in 1975. Even more—$41.9 million—is programmed for

1976. Reportedly, the State Department also will license the commercial sale of arms valued at roughly $200 million. In short, Secretary Kissinger has authored the precise policy calculated to aggravate the risk to Red Sea commerce and to encourage intransigence in Addis.

Some enthusiasts for continued aid to Ethiopia rest part of their case on the allegedly dangerous precedent of an Eritrean victory. It would, they insist, encourage latent secessionist movements throughout Africa. Countries would unravel at a terrible cost in blood and aborted development.

The truth is that we know extraordinarily little about the "teaching effects" of particular moments in the stream of history. The chain of assumptions leading from an Eritrean victory—achieved, of course, after more than a decade of awful suffering—to secessionist struggles elsewhere on the continent is long, complicated, and weak. Will many potential dissidents even be aware of what happened in Ethiopia? If aware, will they appreciate the unique characteristics of the Eritrean case which undoubtedly distinguish it from their own? Will they be more impressed by victory or by its costs? How, on the other hand, will Eritrea affect the minds and programs of governing elites? Conceivably, it might frighten them into a more generous, tension-reducing response to the demands of geographically peripheral or ethnically distinct groups for a fairer share of collective goods. Even if we had some persuasive evidence that Eritrean victory would increase the incidence of secessionist movements, whether the net result would be more costly in human or developmental terms than effective repression by central governments is equally unknown.

Arrayed against the bloody quiddity of Ethiopian policy in Eritrea, the bad-precedent argument is exposed as a mass of airy speculations. Perhaps that is one reason why it enjoys little prominence in official justifications for boosting military assistance and licensing increased cash sales to a government employing brutal and illegal means in pursuit of a morally problematic end.

Somalia

In the rhetoric of justification for current U.S. policy, the Somali rather than the Eritrean threat to Ethiopia's territorial integrity enjoys pride of place. Some American military experts are dubious about the alleged threat. They cite Ethiopia's vast superiority in mobilizable manpower, its almost three-to-one advantage in men under arms, and the sharp disparity between the Somalis' technical

know-how and the sophisticated weapon systems on which their allegedly dangerous capabilities are based. In addition, they would
be operating in terrain which places powerful emphasis on logistical
capabilities, by consensus the weakest link in the Somali armed
forces, which reportedly require Soviet technical assistance down
nearly to the company level.

INCENTIVES TO SOVIET RESTRAINT

Given the degree of their dependence on Soviet equipment and advisers, the Somalis are unlikely to initiate a full-scale conflict without assurances of Soviet support. Support would mean a degree of
involvement the Russians would undoubtedly like to avoid. The
Horn, after all, is not Angola. It is exceedingly difficult to tar the
leftist government of Ethiopia as a Western stooge or a South
African consort. African opinion would be resolutely hostile to an
irridentist adventure challenging the sacred norm of respect for
colonial boundaries, a challenge heightened by the location of
OAU headquarters in Addis Ababa. Involvement would therefore
dissipate the fund of good will, while coincidentally inflaming the
suspicions, earned by the Soviet Union in the course of its Angolan
venture. Chinese predictions of Soviet perfidy would seem fulfilled.

Nor would the Kremlin earn credits among the Arabs to offset
its political costs in Black Africa. Although finally admitted to the
Arab League, Somalia has never enjoyed much Arab support for its
territorial claims. On the contrary, the leading Arab actors in the
OAU have generally championed the integrity of existing frontiers.

In addition to jeopardizing its recently enhanced position in Africa, the Soviet Union would risk serious deterioration in relations,
and conceivably a military confrontation, with the United States.
Soviet leaders are sensible of the conservative tide revealed in the
U.S. presidential primaries and the consequent vulnerability of détente. They must be equally aware that long-standing U.S. ties to
Ethiopia, coupled with the popular interest in the Horn fueled by
the imbroglio over Diego Garcia and the congressional tour of Berbera, would augur intense hostility to Soviet involvement even if in
Angola's wake the administration had not drawn a flamboyant rhe-
torical line against further Soviet armed intervention in Africa.
With that line drawn, the risks increase exponentially.

Remaining aloof from the first stage of a conflict between Somalia and Ethiopia would be a difficult trick for the Kremlin and
might, in any event, leave its interests in considerable jeopardy. In
the first place, war could generate Ethiopian air strikes against Soviet facilities, such as the fighter base near Harghessa, which might
be used by the Somali armed forces; the mere possibility of its use

by Somali planes would encourage a pre-emptive attack. Second, Ethiopian forces might ultimately shatter a Somali offensive thrust, particularly one largely unaided by Soviet technical personnel. If the Dergue exploited its initial triumph by invading Somalia, the Russians would face a grave dilemma: on the one hand, direct involvement with all its costs; on the other, acquiescence in the total defeat of their client, probably followed by expulsion from all those costly facilities. And having failed once as a protector, they might encounter a dearth of alternative clients.

The Soviet Union plainly has much to lose should it fail to prevent a Somali adventure. And it has nothing at all to gain if the war is fought only for control of the burnt Ogaden plains, and nothing worth the risk in the now far more likely event of a tussle over the French Territory of the Afars and the Issas.

It is true that for all the Soviet investment in Berbera, Djibouti's port facilities are vastly superior. A Somali victory over Ethiopian forces, in the wake of French withdrawal, followed by an annexation of the territory might give the Russian navy and air force preferential access to Djibouti. That is the potential gain. The potential costs might appear less than in the case of conflict along the whole Somali-Ethiopian interface because in the territory the chances of a quick, decisive Somali victory are greater. Djibouti itself is far more accessible to Somali than Ethiopian forces. And once occupied, it could serve as a base of operations against Ethiopian reinforcements who would, moreover, have to pass through territory harassed by supporters of the Afar sultan, Ali Mireh Hanfare.

A short, decisive war would facilitate Russian maintenance of a low profile. The risk to the Soviets, however, is that the Ethiopians would respond to defeat in the north by attacks farther south, after first mobilizing numerically superior forces. In that probable event, the Soviet Union might finally confront the dilemma sketched earlier.

Involvement in a prolonged conflict with Ethiopia is not, however, the most serious risk which a Somali campaign against the territory carries for the Soviet Union. Mogadishu may be tempted to strike before independence brings the territory under the mantle of OAU and United Nations Charter non-aggression norms. Even if President Barre and his colleagues moved after independence (perhaps in response to appeals from ethnic Somalis claiming persecution by the Afar-dominated postindependence government), French forces may still be on the scene under a base-rights agreement. However vicarious, involvement in a conflict with a Western state bears an appalling danger of direct confrontation with the United States.

There would be little offsetting promise of gain. For although Djibouti would originally have been far preferable to Berbera as a headquarters site for Soviet forces in the Indian Ocean, given the investment already made at Berbera and elsewhere within Somalia, Djibouti's facilities, particularly its air field, are somewhat redundant. They would, of course, be nice as insurance against improbable political and strategic developments which could encourage an enlarged Soviet presence in the Indian Ocean. Perhaps of larger significance from the perspective of Soviet strategists would be the chance of excluding Western use of Djibouti. But in this case, exclusion seems a decidedly minor blessing to the Russians, since the French are not themselves a serious threat to any plausible Soviet interest in the area and, as earlier noted, U.S. naval forces can operate effectively without benefit of access to Djibouti.

The distribution of potential gains and losses thus militates strongly in favor of a Soviet veto on Somali adventures. But can that veto be exercised without jeopardizing the Soviet position in Somalia? Down on the Horn, the Russians seem trapped in the same kind of dilemma which ultimately catapulted them out of Egypt. There, too, they traded military assistance for facilities. There, too, their client's ends required a change in the status quo which it could not effect without deep Soviet involvement. There, too, involvement threatened confrontation with the United States.

The parallel is by no means perfect. On the Horn, the risk of confrontation with the West is less, the client's capabilities in relation to its antagonist's rather more equal, and the client's need for action considerably less pressing. Unlike President Sadat, President Barre apparently is not spurred by internal political forces to demonstrate rapid progress in capturing the "lost territories."* Moreover, as much as they may yearn for positive achievements, the Somalis may equally fear further reverses. If the Soviets will not now support offensive action, Soviet aid may still be deemed essential to discourage an Ethiopian grab for Djibouti or anti-Somali pogroms by a postindependence government in the Territory. In addition, the steady accumulation of Somali military power as troops become more technically sophisticated creates longer-term potential for uniting the Somali people in the not remarkable event of a collapse of central authority either in Ethiopia, or in Kenya following the

---

*Pressure to act may, however, begin to accumulate if much more time passes without concrete achievements or if the French again rig the referendum in the territory or if the Somalis' sense of opportunity is intensified by a split in the Ethiopian armed forces.

death of Kenyatta. Finally, the Russians enjoy considerable leverage incident to their roles in President Barre's domestic program of
social mobilization and resettlement.

For all these reasons, the Soviet Union may not be forced to
choose between the costs of involvement in a conflict on the Horn
and continued access to its facilities. Then again, it may. Other interested parties cannot, in any event, simply assume that the Russians will reject Somali demands for support if they are made or
that refusal will necessarily prevent the Somalis from acting on
their own and thereafter entangling their patrons in a widening
gyre of violence. There is, as well, the danger of a full-scale war initiated by the Ethiopians in reprisal for Somali-sponsored insurgency
or border probes or in order to pre-empt a suspected Somali strike.
Thus, Somalis and Russians could be drawn, willy-nilly, into a war
both might like to avoid.

Continued U.S. military assistance to Ethiopia may help to
deter the Somalis. On the other hand, it probably promotes Ethiopian hostility to proposals for settlement that mediate reasonably
between the interests of the two countries and may ultimately
encourage an Ethiopian essay in pre-emptive war. Meanwhile, it
facilitates progressively more brutal repression in Eritrea.

For reasons elaborated earlier, if the Eritrean conflict is consid-
ered in isolation, the United States can best satisfy the claims both
of conscience and of strategy by a major effort to promote peaceful
settlement in Eritrea and, that failing, by progressive withdrawal of
military assistance. On what grounds may the Somali threat take
precedence over a morally engaging and politically prudent policy
for Eritrea?

THE U.S. COMMITMENT: CREDIBILITY IS NOT ENOUGH

For more than two decades, behind the conventional facade of exalted rhetoric, the United States and Ethiopia have sustained a
marriage of convenience. Time has eroded whatever charms it may
once have had. The government of Ethiopia no longer exercises a
powerful influence in African councils. The value of Kagnew Station, Ethiopia's strategic dowry, is largely exhausted.

During the years when there was real mutuality of interest, the
United States held firmly to its part of the bargain, paying full value
for goods received. Washington created the modern army promised
to the Emperor but undertook no obligation to maintain that army
forever. At most, one might find a quasi-contractual obligation,
subject to congressional veto, to continue some level of assistance
until the Kagnew lease expires in 1978.

But even if we find such a tacit understanding, there is a powerful case for earlier termination. In Eritrea, the government of Ethiopia is employing American weapons to commit hideous crimes of war. Ethiopian forces, regular and irregular, are trampling on the fundamental principle of discrimination between the civilian population and enemy combatants. Like Mr. Kurtz, the protagonist of Conrad's *Heart of Darkness,* they have lost the sense of moral limits. Their strategy becomes progressively less distinguishable from Kurtz's deranged scrawl: "Exterminate all the brutes."

The desperate expedient of recruiting hordes of undisciplined peasants for a march through Eritrea was the ineffable consummation of military policies instinct with contempt for international legality. The Dergue promised land to the invading peasants; in Eritrea, there are no large tracts of unoccupied arable land. The Dergue could not supply this horde; to survive more than a few days, it would have had to ravage the Eritrean peasantry. Though it has disbanded its ragged levy of crusaders, the Dergue shows evidence neither of remorse nor of commitment to self-restraint. Unless it closes its pipeline to the Ethiopian armed forces, the United States will continue being implicated in barbarous acts. That would seem reason enough to conclude that any residual obligation, legal or moral, owed by the United States to the government of Ethiopia has dissolved.

Neither quasi-legal nor moral obligation as such has assumed prominence in the brief of officials urging continued support of the Dergue regardless of what it does in Eritrea. Nor do they make much, if anything, of Kagnew's slight residual value or of the putative danger to Israel of an "Arabized" Red Sea; most officials, if not all journalists, have finally recognized the superficiality of the strategic assumptions underlying that concern. To the extent that these factors have any persuasive dimension at all, they are dwarfed by the overriding concern with American credibility.

At the base of the credibility argument is the simple notion so jauntily captured in Roosevelt's notorious epigram about Trujillo: "No doubt he's an s.o.b.; but he's our s.o.b." The present government of Ethiopia is "ours" in two senses: first, because it is militarily dependent; second, and primarily, because it is *seen* as a U.S. client, just as Somalia is *seen* as a client of the USSR. Indeed, without the contrast offered by the Soviet-Somali liaison, the U.S.-Ethiopian connection would appear far more problematical.

The connection is not only less functional but also much less cordial than in past years. Having nationalized the bulk of foreign investments and adopted a radical-socialist development strategy with all its associated verbal sauce, the Ethiopians hardly appear as ideological progeny of the United States. In the government-controlled press, the Chinese unmistakably enjoy a more favorable reception. Even the Russians are not clearly subordinated to Uncle Sam as objects of official esteem. In the West as well, the bloom is off the rose. The story of the famine cover-up exposed the seamy underside of Haile Selassie's Ethiopia. Eritrea and the butchery of the oligarchs canceled the initial tendency to celebrate his reforming successors. And the perceptible incipience of Western amity with the Islamic world coinciding roughly with the severing of Ethiopia's Israeli connection has reduced, albeit not eliminated, a reflexive concern for the Christian island in its Islamic sea. So if the Somalis were not reddened with the Soviet brush, the vision of Ethiopia as a natural, almost hereditary friend whose peril must create a test of American will would surely be blurred.

Secretary Kissinger has been criticized for conjuring challenges where, but for his Spenglerian rhetoric, none would have been apparent to the reasonable man's naked eye. The secretary's taste for hyperbole invites this line of attack, for his florid warnings obscure the established tracks of rhetoric and policy along which he chuffs. After all, neither Kissinger nor Nixon invented the rationale for burrowing ever deeper into the quagmire of Vietnam: "It may have been a mistake to go there, but now that we are there we must stay." Nor is it fair to say that this American obsession with credibility is self-generating. In fact, it is regularly reinforced by frightened voices from our various security dependencies, large and small.

Despite occasional sneers from the Left, credibility with friend and foe alike is unquestionably a legitimate concern. We do not want to mislead the Russians into adventures which could inadvertently produce a perilous confrontation. Nor, for various reasons, do we want allies to doubt our willingness to meet our commitments.

It is not a concern with American credibility that is the proper object of criticism; rather, it is the failure to define commitments in ways which reflect accurately the material and moral interests of the United States and its principal allies. Soviet support for one side in a struggle is an insufficient reason to discover a U.S. commitment to the other side. To act as if it were is perversely to allow U.S. policy to be made in Moscow. Yet, we have sometimes seemed to allow precisely that. Where the result is association with the destiny of factions or regimes pursuing heinous ends or employing barbarous means or demonstrating relative incompetence to do anything at all, as the case may be, credibility becomes an end in itself, de-

manding the perpetuation of initial error. When the result is suffi-
ciently costly or morally grotesque, the national will not unrea-
sonably flags.

Ethiopia can be distinguished on easily understood grounds
from cases in which the United States has real commitments the
prolongation of which is in the national interest. Washington is
bound to Addis by neither a mutual defense treaty nor shared strategic benefits nor a common ideology nor American investments
nor ascriptive ties between Ethiopians and some segment of our own
population. What ties, if any, have survived the long marriage of
convenience are offset by the use of American aid for the conduct of
flagrantly illegal activities. However, in light of the counterinsurgency record of the United States, invocation of atrocities in
Eritrea as a basis for dissociation will be far more convincing if the
U.S. government coincidentally concedes past error and commits
itself to the same standards used to judge Ethiopia.

Aside from invoking the putative erosion of American credibility in the event a Soviet client is allowed to whip a country traditionally associated with the United States, some supporters of the
State Department's current policy line advance the peril of conflict
spreading beyond the borders of Ethiopia and Somalia. There are
conceivable scenarios to support this concern. *If* Somalia succeeded
in annexing the Ogaden, it might then turn its attention to Kenya's
Northern Frontier District (NFD). *And if* renewed pressure on the
Kenyans led ultimately to war, possibly the Somalis might successfully urge Idi Amin, the belligerent Muslim dictator of Uganda, to
open a second front against Kenya. Then Julius Nyerere, bitter
enemy of Amin, might cast his lot with Kenya. Ethiopia, eager for
revenge, might join in too.

Anything is conceivable. But would Somali victory in a war with
Ethiopia, catalyzed by the withdrawal of U.S. support, enhance the
plausibility of this particular scenario? Arguably, a strong Ethiopia
may ultimately deflect Somali ambitions toward the NFD. Or a
temporarily defeated Ethiopia might exhaust Somali military
energy by slowly gathering its strength along the new border which
would stretch Somali supply lines. Actually, the event most likely to
precipitate Somali intervention in Kenya is internal conflict following the death of Kenyatta, not victory or stalemate in the contest
with Ethiopia.

Ethiopia's military preponderance on the Horn might deter Somali intervention. But its preponderance is gone and will not be restored by the U.S. aid and sales now envisioned. Hence, they seem
to bear little rational relationship to the alleged danger.

THE PROSPECT FOR ACCOMMODATION

The risks possibly associated with U.S. termination of arms transfers to Ethiopia could be avoided altogether if, either alone or in conjunction with the Soviet Union, we could arrange a settlement between Ethiopia and Somalia. Is there any basis for accommodation?

The Emperor was right. The Horn of Africa is a natural economic unit. Its political subdivisions are potentially symbiotic. Development in the hinterland could foster prosperity in the Indian Ocean, as well as the Red Sea, ports. If large oil or gas reserves rest under the soil of the Ogaden, their most economic path to the sea is through Somalia. Neither the Somalis nor the Ethiopians can rationalize their meat-packing operations without cooperative pricing policies designed to assure a predictable flow of animals to slaughter houses. Realization of the full agricultural potential of the land adjacent to the Juba and Wabi-Shebelle rivers, the only large cultivable area in Somalia, probably requires an interstate compact since the rivers rise in Ethiopia. Without close cooperation, neither government can do very much to ameliorate the nomads' increasingly tortured existence.

Nevertheless, accommodation of the Somali-Ethiopian conflict appears in most respects even more difficult than an Eritrean settlement. In the first place, the amount of territory involved is much greater; almost one-fifth of Ethiopia is inhabited by Somali clans and thus subject to claims for "self-determination." Second, there is some evidence that it contains commercial reserves of natural gas and, possibly, oil. Third, the precedent of territorial secession could not be isolated nearly as easily, since the larger part of Somali-occupied land was at least nominally incorporated within Ethiopia's domain a half-century before the end of the colonial era at the same time as non-Somali territories in the southern part of the country. Fourth, Ethiopians are accustomed to viewing the Somalis as a long-term security threat; they are likely to regard any territories, however impoverished, transferred to Somalia as an enhancement of Somali power. Finally, there are no elements in Somali society, analogous to the Eritrean Christians and Eritrean members of the imperial civil and military services, with a vested interest in some organic political relationship with Ethiopia that could, as in the Eritrean case, neutralize the cankerous issue of sovereignty. The only distinction favorable to settlement is the "cold" character of the conflict. Neither side has wasted the land or decimated the population of the other. They do not, therefore, possess such deep reserves of hatred and guilt.

The obstacles to settlement may be insurmountable. If they can be overcome, as in the Eritrean case it can be managed only by jettisoning conventionally rigid notions of territorial sovereignty in favor of a more fluid and functional architecture of political authority. To use the normal legal argot, both sides must accept some overlap of national jurisdiction. The overlap might be limited to the disputed territories or might embrace all of the two states through some form of confederation that would include special treatment for the Somali-speaking inhabitants of Ethiopia.

The former approach could be modeled after the Anglo-Ethiopian agreement which theoretically allowed the British to exercise authority in Ethiopian territory over nomads from the British Protectorate. Ethiopia and Somalia might agree that all the Somali-speaking inhabitants of the eastern frontier area could opt either for Ethiopian or Somali citizenship. They might further agree to maintain an open border so that, regardless of citizenship, people could move freely and settle throughout both countries. Persons accused of crimes in one state would be subject to extradition in the other. Somali citizens might be exempted from Ethiopian taxation but, on the other hand, would have to pay user fees for local services.

The courts, the administration, and the police would be staffed to the fullest feasible extent by indigenous personnel. The border would be permanently demilitarized, and each party would agree not to station troops within a certain distance of it.

The oil and gas issue could be resolved by the designation of a joint development area on *both sides* of the frontier to the depth of a prescribed number of miles. Title to all oil and gas reserves would be assigned to a public corporation, established by treaty, in which the two states would hold equal shares. This arrangement would not constitute a unilateral Ethiopian concession. The geological formations on the Somali side of the provisional border are not notably different from those in the Ogaden. Such reserves as there may be seem as likely to be found on one side of the frontier as on the other. An agreement on joint development would, in addition, assure access to the sea along the most economic route for a pipeline. Finally, it should be noted that the now most promising exploration area inside Ethiopia is located in that part of the Ogaden where Somalia has the strongest legal claims to a favorable adjustment.

As long as Ethiopia remained a Coptic autocracy with a medieval social structure, there was no basis for voluntary political association with Somalia. A truly secularized and socialist Ethiopia should open new vistas of cooperation. One, of course, concedes that, however compatible their domestic programs, the leaders of these two countries are still the heirs of ancient enmities and ambitions. Moreover, without such a heritage, socialism (scientific or otherwise) has proven, in Africa and elsewhere, perfectly compatible with fanatic forms of nationalism. It is nevertheless true that, other things being not too unequal, convergent social systems tend to foster cooperation.

The proposed secularization of Ethiopian society—lent early authenticity by the Dergue's proclamation of Mohammed's birthday as a national holiday—also could facilitate a Somali-Ethiopian accord. The Coptic church has been the historic bearer of Ethiopian particularism and a powerful supporter of cultural intolerance. On this score, too, there are signs of convergence. Despite President Barre's insistence on the compatibility of his political program with traditional Islam—a religion whose devotees have, on occasion, been no less intolerant than their Abyssinian counterparts—promulgation of equal rights for women reinforced the discernible impulse to subordinate religion to the canons of modernization.

With its independence probably less than a year away, the Territory of the Afars and the Issas becomes a vital element in any scheme of accommodation. Simple neutralization will not do. President Barre and his colleagues regard the area between Djibouti and the border as a historic part of the Somali domain, dismembered by imperialist treachery. The minimum they will settle for is a referendum, conducted by the United Nations or the OAU, in which Somalis traditionally resident in the area can participate. If the thousands of Somalis expelled by the French were allowed to return and vote, a Somali-dominated political coalition might win. And it, in turn, might opt for association with the Somali Democratic Republic, a result which would probably be regarded by the Ethiopians as nothing less than a *casus belli*.

An agreement dividing the territory between its neighbors but establishing a condominium over Djibouti guaranteed by the OAU or actually converting Djibouti into a free port under the auspices of the OAU might accommodate Ethiopian and Somali interests but would probably be anathema to the Afars. Nevertheless, if an arrangement along these lines satisfied Addis and Mogadishu, the OAU probably would ignore Afar complaints.

The surest way to make oneself an object of scorn among hardened diplomats is to propose terms of settlement for an interstate dispute which require more than incremental change in the behavior of the antagonists. It is hard to arraign their cynicism, forged as it so obviously is on the anvil of experience. If history is any guide, most states most of the time would rather fight than change. And the hardest change of all to contemplate in this era of resurgent nationalism, sanctioned by the charter and practice of the United Nations, is one involving the very definition of the state.

Nevertheless, there are occasions when, through some extraordinary conjunction of circumstances, states are propelled out of their normal behavioral orbits. Though always unique, the circumstantial pattern undoubtedly includes in its constituents a sensation of newly released, momentous, and transient possibilities. That describes the state of the Horn today. In Ethiopia, a form of state and society, the essence of which congealed a millennium ago, is being smashed apart. The Somali leadership is attempting to recast equally ancient forms of social life. These efforts occur against a backdrop of stunning change in the surrounding international environment.

The fact remains, however, that neither side has yet demonstrated any impulse to settlement. On the contrary, tension continues to build while Ethiopia accuses its neighbor of preparing an invasion. As in the case of Eritrea, a strong push from external forces probably is required if the belligerents are likely even to contemplate compromise.

Given the danger to Soviet interests latent in the prevailing tension between Somalia and Ethiopia, the Russians should be sympathetic to the idea of accommodation unless a U.S. demarche is seen as one element in a scheme to expel them from the Horn. A settlement along the lines just proposed would necessarily reduce but it would hardly dissolve the vast historical residue of mutual competition and suspicion. Nor would it resolve the question of the Somalis of Kenya. As the naturally weaker state, Somalia would feel a particular need to maintain relatively strong armed forces. A competent army would moderate the risk and provide insurance against the consequences of renewed tension while reinforcing the influence in African councils of this poor, thinly populated country. Furthermore, the army would remain the backbone of the regime and the engine of social mobilization. For all of these reasons, the Somalis will continue to require large-scale military assistance. What the Russians may fear, however, is that accommodation will make it easier for the United States to threaten the principal basis of their position in Somalia by offering itself as an alternative source of aid.

The Russians are, therefore, unlikely to support an effort to promote accommodation unless the United States is prepared informally to accept their presence in Somalia as a legitimate occasion of the superpower game.* That is not an onerous condition.

---

*The U.S. might usefully link such acceptance to a more explicit understanding than the one which may now exist with respect to dimensions and functions of naval deployments in the Indian Ocean.

For the reasons listed earlier, the United States is likely to accrue only a small, and in any event, transient advantage from Russian expulsion. Hence, the costs of replacing them as a fertile source of military and economic aid would be very hard to justify.

Once their fears about the security of their facilities are allayed, the Russians should be inclined to cooperate both in the hope of avoiding the outbreak of a potentially hazardous conflict and, perhaps, to reinforce the beleaguered American advocates of détente. But given the primacy of its strategic investment in Somalia, the Soviet Union's cooperation almost certainly will not assume the form of pressure on its Somali hosts. The Russians might advise the Somalis to accept a solution short of annexation, and they might offer still larger dollops of aid as an incentive. But they cannot be expected to threaten reduced aid levels in case the Somalis prove intransigent. If, as it should, the United States terminates military assistance to avoid complicity with Ethiopian policy in Eritrea, the Ethiopians will be equally immune to negative incentives, since even a willingness to compromise with the Somalis would not, on this assumption, avoid the withdrawal of aid.

Assuming that, for their respective reasons, the two superpowers cannot use sticks to bludgeon their clients into an agreement, there is still the carrot of increased economic support. Ethiopia and particularly Somalia are already recipients of petrodollar largesse. Under the aegis of the United States, both regimes might receive a substantial step-up in assistance from conservative Arab governments. To increase its leverage, the assistance could be earmarked for joint development projects. With the cooperation of one or more of the major oil companies, the United States could further enhance the charms of accommodation by facilitating accelerated exploration of the area's oil and gas potential. Faced, on the one hand, with the irremedial loss of American support and, on the other, with positive financial incentives, the Dergue might reveal a hitherto unsuspected pliancy. Financial incentives, coupled with the perceived risk that central authority in Ethiopia not only will survive its present crisis but will succeed in strengthening itself by transforming society, may similarly wean the Somalis from the full measure of their irridentist dreams to a negotiated settlement.

Accommodation is conceivable, it is desirable, and it should be attempted. But the balance of probability is against success. Hence, while pursuing accommodation, the architects of policy must prepare designs for the contingency of failure. If Somalis and Ethiopians cling to their historic enmity, the odds favor war on the Horn of Africa. And if war comes, the odds will even more heavily favor the further unraveling of détente.

Epilogue:
The Phenomenology of Crisis

A private eye, commisioned to discover what happened to Mrs. X, provides satisfaction to his principal regardless of what he finds. Whether she has been dismembered or is merely backpacking in the Rockies is irrelevant to his fee, his future, or his job-related gratification. In theory, perhaps, the strategist should be equally free of an impulse to find soluble trouble. Yet, in the real world, the announcement that no problem exists or, if it does, that it has no solution tends to leave all concerned with a feeling that time, energy, and money have been wasted. Why?

Because the *raison d'être* of the private eye's principal is not solving problems of the kind investigated. A government, on the other hand, has no other purpose. If you tell it that there is no basis for intervention, either because some problem is beyond the reach of diplomacy or because in country Y or region Z one outcome is not more consequential than another, that events can or should be left alone, the principal's reason for being is to that degree diminished.

The analyst's sense of his own value is also diminished, even if he has no formal relationship to his or any other potentially concerned government, because if he is persuasive, his study will be forgotten. If, on the other hand, he finds a potential crisis requiring continued concern and action, his study is transformed into a guide. It lives as long as it is used.

Private investigators do not expect their work to have resonance. Each investigation is a series of acts which, when completed, vanish. Strategic studies, however, have a potential life which dawns when they are completed. But their life span is a function, often, of the potential calamities they forecast. It would not, therefore, be incredible if a man, sent by the Schlunk Center for Strategic Studies to examine developments in, shall we say, Andorra, were more inclined to entitle his work "Andorra: Strategic Magnet of the 1990s" than "Andorra: From Triviality to Irrelevance." Nor would it be incredible if he spoke ominously of communist penetration of the gourd-growers union, noted that the country stands at one of the choke points of Spanish tourism, and warned that if the point were choked it could lead to massive intervention by enraged drivers.

I have tried to resist the incentive to overdramatize. Since, for those who can see beyond the end of a geometer's compass, the Horn's strategic significance is relatively slight, I was inclined initially to write it off as a potential environment for international crisis. That, however, was before Angola, before the perceptible backlash from U.S. failure in Vietnam, before the denigration of American willpower became a full-fledged intellectual industry. And it was, as well, before the French threatened to open the tinderbox of the Territory of the Afars and the Issas.

If war comes to the Horn, even through spontaneous combustion or Ethiopian pre-emption rather than a Somali initiative, the Russians cannot avoid the appearance of complicity. Unless public opinion is alerted to the parochial roots of the conflict and the limited influence the superpowers can reasonably exert on their "clients," the prevailing skepticism — and in certain sectors outright hostility — towards the incipient process of U.S.-Soviet accommodation and the compulsion to demonstrate U.S. willpower are likely to cement diverse American constituencies in a demand for aid to Ethiopia and coercive measures against Somalia's patron. They will, as well, conspire to obscure the distinctly local causes of the conflict and the autonomous will of the belligerents, while bootlessly inflating the strategic value of the area. Advocates of intervention will caricature the Somalis as puppets dangling on Soviet strings and the Ethiopians as doughty underdogs defending a noble tradition and a sacred principle of international law. We can anticipate rhetorical invocation of the 1930s with Ethiopia playing again the improbable role of Western democracy's hero. And, as for détente, it will again be victimized by the inertial force of a global competition which neither superpower yet knows how to reduce.

Crises, like beauty, exist not in the nature of things but in the minds of men. They arise at peculiar conjunctions of time, place, and circumstance. In the wake of Vietnam, the air is filled with tests of will looking for somewhere to settle. The Horn is not an especially hospitable setting for human habitation. But as a venue for confrontation by proxy, it now shows real promise.

Bibliography

Abir, Mordechai. "The Contentious Horn of Africa." *Conflict Studies* 23 (June 1972).

_____, "Red Sea Politics" in *Conflicts in Africa. Adelphi Papers Number Ninety-three*. London: The International Institute for Strategic Studies, 1972.

_____. "The Reopening of the Suez Canal — Strategic Aspects." *Israel Defense Army Quarterly,* May 1974.

_____. "Sharm al-Sheikh — Bab al-Mandeb: The Strategic Balance and Israel's Southern Approaches." *Jerusalem Papers on Peace Problems.* Jerusalem: The Hebrew University, 1974.

Atkins, Harry. *A Geography of Ethiopia*. Addis Ababa: Sim Printing Press, 1970.

Bell, J. Bowyer. "Bab El Mandeb, Strategic Troublespot." *Orbis* 16 (Winter 1973).

_____. "Endemic Insurgency and International Order: The Eritrea Experience." *Orbis* 18 (Summer 1974).

_____. *The Horn of Africa: Strategic Magnet in the Seventies*. New York: Crane Russak & Co., 1973.

_____. "Strategic Implications of Soviet Presence in Somalia." *Orbis* 19 (Summer 1975).

Burrell, R.M. "The USSR and the Indian Ocean." *Soviet Analyst,* March 11, 1974.

Campbell, John Franklin. "Background to the Eritrean Conflict.' *Africa Report* 16 (May 1971).

Castagne, A. A. "Interview with Mohamed Siad Barre." *Africa Report* 16 (December 1971).

_____. "Somalia Goes Military." *Africa Report* 15 (February 1970).

Clapham, C. "Ethiopia and Somalia" in *Conflicts in Africa. Adelphi*

Papers Number Ninety-three. London: The International Institute for Strategic Studies, 1972.

Cohen, J. M. "Ethiopia After Haile Selassie: The Government Land Factor." *African Affairs* 72 (October 1973).

Contini, Jeanne. "The Illiterate Poets of Somalia." *Reporter,* March 14, 1963.

Cottrell, Alvin J. and R. M. Burrell. "Soviet-U.S. Naval Competition in the Indian Ocean." *Orbis* 18 (Winter 1974).

Cox, David R. "Sea Power and Soviet Foreign Policy." *U.S. Naval Institute Proceedings* 95 (June 1969).

Decraene, Philippe. "Scientific Socialism — African Style." *Africa Report* 20 (May-June 1975).

Democratic Republic of Somalia, *Memorandum on French Somaliland to the U.N. Special Committee on the Situation with Regard to the Implementation of the Declaration on the Granting of Independence to Colonial Territories and Peoples,* Ministry of Foreign Affairs, June 1, 1965.

Drysdale, John. *The Somali Dispute*. New York: Praeger, 1964.

Enahoro, Peter. "Eritrea's War of Secession." *Africa,* March 1975.

"Ethiopia: Land War." *Africa,* December 1975.

"Ethiopia: The Military Regime." *Africa Confidential* 15 (September 20, 1974).

"Ethiopian Tikden." *Africa,* April 1975.

Great Britain, Colonial Office. *Kenya: Report of the Northern Frontier District Commission* (CMND, 1900), London: HMSO, 1962.

Greenfield, Richard; Perham, Dame Margerie; Levine, Donald N. *Ethiopia: A New Political History*. New York: Praeger, 1965.

Halliday, Fred. "The Fighting in Eritrea." *New Left Review* 67 (May-June 1971).

Jaffe, Andrew. "Haile Selassie's Remarkable Reign." *Africa Report* 16 (May 1971).

Jane's Fighting Ships. New York: Franklin Watts, Inc., 1975-76.

Jukes, Geoffrey. *The Indian Ocean in Soviet Naval Policy. Adelphi Papers Number Eighty-Seven*. London: The International Institute for Strategic Studies, 1972.

Kaplan, Irving *et al. Area Handbook for Ethiopia*. Washington, D.C.: American University Foreign Area Studies, 1971.

Legum, Colin. "Ethiopia Looks for Reformers." *Observer Foreign News Service,* July 5, 1974.

——————. "Ethiopia Losing Hope of Winning Eritrean War." *Observer Foreign News Service,* July 9, 1974.

——————. "Ethiopia's Army Split by Feuds." *Observer Foreign News Service,* July 4, 1974.

_____. "Ethiopia's Soldiers Ready to Fill Power Vacuum." *Observer Foreign News Service,* July 3, 1974.

Levine, Donald. *Greater Ethiopia.* Chicago: University of Chicago Press, 1965.

_____. "The Roots of Ethiopia's Nationhood." *Africa Report* 16 (May 1971).

_____. *Wax and Gold.* Chicago: University of Chicago Press, 1965.

Lewis, Ian M. *The Modern History of Somaliland.* New York: Praeger, 1965.

_____. ""The Referendum in French Somaliland: Aftermath and Prospects in the Somali Dispute." *World Today* 23 (July 23, 1967).

Manning, Robert. "Diego Garcia: The Pentagon Trump Card." *Far Eastern Economic Review* 90 (November 7, 1975).

Matatu, Godwin. "Interview with Mohamed Said." *Africa,* April 1975.

MccGwire, Michael, ed. *Soviet Naval Developments: Capability and Context.* New York: Praeger, 1973.

McConnell, James M. and Anne M. Kelly. "Super-Power Naval Diplomacy: Lessons of the Indo-Pakistani Crisis 1971." *Survival* 15 (November-December 1973).

Marks, Thomas A. "Djibouti: France's Strategic Toehold in Africa." *African Affairs* 73 (January 1974).

Martin, L. "The New Power Gap in the Indian Ocean." *Interplay* 3 (January 1969).

Matthies, Volker. "The Horn of Africa and International Relations." *Intereconomics* 12 (December 1974).

Meister, Jurg. "Diego Garcia: Outpost in the Indian Ocean." *Swiss Review of World Affairs,* April 1974.

The Military Balance 1975-1976. London: The International Institute for Strategic Studies, 1975.

Millar, T. B. *The Indian and Pacific Oceans: Some Strategic Considerations. Adelphi Papers Number Fifty-Seven.* London: The International Institute for Strategic Studies, 1972.

_____. "Soviet Policies South and East of Suez." *Foreign Affairs* 49 (October 1970).

Moorehead, Alan. *The Blue Nile.* New York: Harper & Row, 1962.

Mousset, Paul. "Referendum à Djibouti." *Revue des Deux Mondes,* April 15, 1967.

Oudes, Bruce. "The Lion of Judah and the Lambs of Washington." *Africa Report* 20 (May-June 1975).

Pankhurst, Richard K. *State and Land in Ethiopian History.* Addis Ababa: Institute of Ethiopian Studies, 1966.

Perham, Dame Margerie. *The Government of Ethiopia*. London: Faber & Faber, 1969.

"Reopening the Suez Canal." *The Petroleum Economist* 41 (December 1974).

Robbs, P. "Battle for the Red Sea." *Africa Report* 20 (March-April 1975).

Schroeder, Richard C. "Indian Ocean Policy." *Editorial Research Reports,* March 10, 1970.

Shepherd, Jack. *The Politics of Starvation*. New York: Carnegie Endowment for International Peace, 1975.

Shilling, Nancy A. "Problems of Political Development in a Ministate: The French Territory of the Afars and Issas." *Journal of Developing Areas* 7 (July 1973).

Singh, K. R. *Politics of the Indian Ocean*. New Delhi: Thompson Press Ltd., 1974.

Spencer, John. "Haile Selassie: Triumph and Tragedy." *Orbis* 18 (Winter 1975).

Thomas, Hugh S. "Not-so Vital Suez Canal." *New York Times Magazine,* March 17, 1974.

Thompson, Virginia and Richard Adloff. *Djibouti and the Horn of Africa*. Stanford, California: Stanford University Press, 1968.

Touval, Saadia. *Somali Nationalism*. Cambridge, Massachussetts: Harvard University Press, 1960.

Trevaskis, G. K. N. *Eritrea, A Colony in Transition*. London: Oxford University Press, 1960.

United Nations, General Assembly, Ad Hoc Committee on the Indian Ocean, *Declaration of the Indian Ocean as a Zone of Peace* (A/AC 159/1), May 3, 1974.

United Nations, General Assembly, *Report of the U.N. Commission for Eritrea* (Fifth Session, Supplement Number Eight-A/1285), 1950.

United Nations, General Assembly, *Resolution 390 A (V) : Final Report of the United Nations Commission in Eritrea* (Seventh Session, Supplement Number Fifteen A/2188), 1950.

United Nations, Conference on Trade and Development, 1973, *The Economic Effects of the Closure of the Suez Canal* (TD/B/C.4/104/ Rev. 1).

Unna, Warren. "Diego Garcia." *New Republic,* March 9, 1974.

U.S. Congress, House, *Hearings on the Proposed Expansion of U.S. Military Facilities in the Indian Ocean Before the Subcommittee on the Near East and South Asia of the House Committee on Foreign Affairs,* 93rd Cong., 2nd sess., 1974.

Weinland, R.G. "The Changing Mission of the Soviet Navy." *Survival* 14 (May-June 1972).

Whitaker, B., ed. *The Fourth World*. New York: Schocken Books, 1972.